WHAT YOU SHOULD KNOW ABOUT

JEWISH RELIGION
HISTORY, ETHICS
AND CULTURE

what you should know about

JEWISH RELIGION, HISTORY, ETHICS AND CULTURE

by

Rabbi Sidney L. Markowitz

THE CITADEL PRESS

SECAUCUS, NEW JERSEY

ABOUT THE AUTHOR

Rabbi Sidney L. Markowitz is a distinguished educator as well as spiritual leader. A former lecturer and advisor at Touro College, he is a member of the Jewish Educators Assembly, has belonged to the American Federation of School Administrators, and was Executive Vice-President of the Hebrew Principals Association of the State of New York. He is a member of the Authors' Guild of America and is the author of *Jewish Holidays and Festivals, Prayer for a Day, Israel, the Eternal Land, Jewish Symbols and Customs,* a collection of folk stories, and twenty-three study workbooks for classroom use. He has also translated a number of articles from Russian, Hebrew, and Yiddish into English.

Copyright © 1955, 1982 by Citadel Press
All rights reserved
Published by Citadel Press
A division of Lyle Stuart Inc.
120 Enterprise Avenue, Secaucus, N.J. 07094
Pubished in Canada by Musson Book Company
A Division of General Publishing Co. Limited
Don Mills, Ontario
Manufactured in the United States of America
ISBN 0-8065-0811-6

ACKNOWLEDGMENTS

The author is most grateful to the following for the encouragement, advice and practical help he received in preparing this book:

Mr. Jacob Goldenkoff, prominent New York attorney; Mr. Boris Kagan, Zionist leader and educator; Rabbi Hersh Kohn, Congregation Tifereth Israel of Riverside, New York City; Mr. Arthur Lessac, Director of the Institute for Research in Voice and Speech, New York; Mr. M. L. Markson, Principal, Temple Adath Israel, New York City, and Instructor at Yeshiva Soloveitchik.

FOR WHOM THIS BOOK IS WRITTEN

For Jews of all shades of opinion: It is amazing how little we know of our own traditions, culture and background. Too many of us have been laboring under distortions, illusions and superficial explanations tantamount to immature superstitions.

For the inquisitive child and curious youth: Youngsters, not knowing the real background of Jewish symbols and customs, cannot evaluate them and have no way of comparing them with the symbols and customs of other people.

For parents: Here they will find the information necessary to answer the ceaseless questions asked by their children.

For non-Jews, who want a clear, realistic picture of Jewish religious, historical and social life: This objective knowledge will contribute to better understanding between Jew and non-Jew.

For the classroom, youth centers, summer camps, or army camps.

CONTENTS

PART TWO
JEWISH RELIGION, ETHICS AND CULTURE

APPENDIX

Part One

JEWISH HISTORY

(See Addenda, p. 223, for Highlights in the History of Israel)

CHAPTER ONE

JEWISH SOCIAL, RELIGIOUS
AND POLITICAL MOVEMENTS

The first part of this book includes not only brief accounts of the acting principals in Jewish history, but also their activity in the religious and political movements which they have created and in which they participated. It includes an account of modern times, in which two of the greatest segments of the Jewish nation, namely the United States and Israel, are molding the modern culture of the Jewish nation.

Some readers may wonder, where did the ancestors of the Torah people, before Abraham, the first Hebrew, come from?

In the first two sections of Genesis, the Pentateuch gives a brief account of happenings from Creation to Abraham, including the flood, the Tower of Babel, the gradual development of civilization from a nomadic state to an agricultural one. As described in the Bible, these ancestors were Arameans, who were nomadic shepherds, came from Ur and settled in Haran (Mesopotamia). They took part in the great Chaldean Civilization. However, a segment of that tribe of Terah, under the leadership of his son Abraham, moved to the South, to live their own life. They created an entirely new belief in one God, and revolutionized the whole world with that belief.

For a while, during the days of Isaac, Jacob, Joseph and his brothers, there took place some personal family disagreements between members of the tribe, like between Isaac and Ishmael, his brother; Jacob and Esau; Joseph and his brothers; but they were personal quarrels only, as the family was small (as it is told in the Bible that only seventy people came to Egypt with Jacob). Ideological and sociological ideas began to clash and became national movements only in the days of Moses, after the Exodus from Egypt of close to a million people, including also slaves of other nationalities (The Erev Rav, great intermixture). Our first chapter begins with the first such difference of opinion, culminating in two parties in the desert, fighting for their ideas for close to forty years. The chapter continues with different Jewish political, religious and social movements down to our time.

IN THE DESERT (*1300 B.C.E., which means Before Common Era*)

Political life in the desert was expressed by two parties, whose basic desires for the future of the Jews differed sharply. One, the Freedom Party, advocated a life of independence by invading and conquering the promised land of Canaan. The other, or Pro-Egyptian party advocated a return to Egypt. The Pro-Egyptian group which was a source of trouble to Moses, was eliminated during the forty years of wandering in the desert.

IN THE DAYS OF JUDGES (*1260-1067 B.C.E.*)

After the death of Joshua, there were two opposed political trends. The one which prevailed opposed unity of the tribes. It was dominated by the heads of the tribes of Judah and Ephraim, who were rivals for national leadership. The minority advocated a united nation under one ruler. For nearly

16

two hundred years, until the days of Samuel, the tribes were independent of each other, uniting only in time of emergency.

IN THE DAYS OF SAMUEL (*1100 B.C.E.*)

During Samuel's rule as a judge, he succeeded in uniting the twelve tribes. When Samuel grew old, and his two sons proved incompetent and dishonest, the demand for a king became insistent. Samuel, however, felt that only God should be king and ruler. For this reason he led a small minority which advocated the formation of a republic.

The majority demanded a king, and Samuel, with God's advice, chose Saul as a ruler.

IN THE DAYS OF SAUL (*1067 B.C.E.*)

Saul's reign, and the period after his death, found two factions fighting for control of Israel. There was the house of Saul and the house of David. As long as Saul was alive, David was a fugitive. When Saul and his three sons were killed in battle with the Philistines, David returned. He became king, but only over the tribe of Judah. The remainder of Israel was under the nominal rule of Ish-Bosheth, a son of Saul. Ish-Bosheth was but a pawn in the hands of General Abner, his military commander-in-chief. After seven and a half years, when he had strengthened his rule, and Abner had been killed, David was made king of all Israel.

SECESSION MOVEMENT (*975 B.C.E.*)

The historical rivalry between the tribes of Ephraim and Judah did not abate. The secessionists, under the leadership of Jeroboam, revolted against Solomon (who was from the tribe of Judah), but were put to flight. Jeroboam fled to Egypt to await a more opportune time. When Solomon died and his son, the haughty and foolish Rehoboam became king, Jeroboam succeeded in getting ten tribes to form a separate kingdom under the name of Israel. He then became their first king. Thus, the great kingdom which David and Solomon had built, was divided.

DURING FIRST TEMPLE (975-586 B.C.E.)

During the first Temple, political opinion was divided among the Pro-Aramean, the Pro-Assyrian, and the Pro-Egyptian groups. In Israel the prophets warned against foreign entanglements, but the rulers ignored them and the result was conquest by Assyria. In Judea there first developed Pro-Assyrian and Pro-Egyptian groups, and later a Pro-Babylonian group. A small minority, led by the prophet Isaiah and later Jeremiah, advocated neutrality. The rulers ignored the advice and entered an alliance with Egypt against Babylon. The result was the conquest of Judea by Babylon.

IN THE DAYS OF EZRA AND NEHEMIAH (5th century B.C.E.)

After Babylon was overthrown by the Persians, the Jews were given permission to return to Judea. The majority of the Jews who lived in Babylon at that time, remained there and became prosperous. A very small minority, under the leadership of Ezra and Nehemiah, a tiny group of three to four hundred returned. This tiny, but determined group won the battle for Judea by building a new life there.

IN THE DAYS OF THE MACCABEES (160 B.C.E.)

In the days of the Maccabees, there were again two parties in Judea. The Hellenists under the leadership of Jason, advocated the adoption of Greek customs; and the Hasidim under the leadership of Matathias and his five sons, advocated the preservation of Jewish customs undiluted by Greek infusions. Although the Hasidim (the Maccabees) were in the minority, their heroism, steadfast faith and brilliant leadership, won religious freedom and political freedom for the Jews. The holiday of Chanukah is celebrated each year in memory of this event, and the Maccabees take their place in history beside all the fighters for freedom.

HYRKAN AND ARISTOBULUS (*1st Century B.C.E.*)

After the death of queen Shlomith Alexandra of the house of the Hasmoneans (the dynasty established by the Maccabees), her two sons began a fight for power. Hyrkan, and his treacherous Edomite adviser, Antipater, favored the Romans. Aristobulus favored an independent policy and did not trust Rome's friendship. Hyrkan invited the Romans to help him against his own brother. Pompey, the Roman Consul, took advantage of this to put an end to Judean independence.

POLITICAL AND RELIGIOUS PARTIES IN JUDEA BEFORE THE DESTRUCTION OF THE SECOND TEMPLE (*1st Century B.C.E.*)

There were three religious, semi-political parties in Judea at that time, as well as two political parties. They were:

THE PHARISEES (from the word Parush—to separate) who consisted of the bulk of the laity and the poor.

The Pharisees advocated:
1. The country to be governed by laws of Torah.
2. The laws of Sages to be respected as laws of Torah.

3. The Jews should be moral example for other nations.
4. The Jews should not adopt the customs of Romans.
5. Belief in life after death.
6. Belief in equality of all people before God.
7. Popular education.
8. Liberal interpretation of Torah.
9. Synagogue organization.
10. Development of liturgy.

THE SADDUCEES (after originator—Zadok) who consisted of the wealthy, priestly class.

The Sadducees advocated:

1. Civil law above religious law.
2. Conversion of non-Jews to Judaism by force, if necessary.
3. Strict interpretation of the Torah.
4. Disregard for Oral law (Talmud).
5. Strict Temple worship with animal sacrifice.
6. Disregard for belief in Resurrection.

THE ESSENES (from the Aramaic: Asiah—healer), who were fishermen and farmers.

The Essenes advocated:

1. Ascetic life.
2. Celibacy.
3. Strict observance of law.
4. Simple life.
5. Communal joint ownership of property.
6. Daily communal immersion.
7. Wearing of white clothes.

8. Praying together.
9. Practicing religion together.
10. No meat or wine to be consumed.
11. Silence during prayer or meal.

THE ZEALOTS (or Independence party) consisted of many young Jews who were against Roman rule.

The Independence party or the Zealots advocated a fight to the finish. Rome, with its superior numbers, emerged victorious. Simon Bar Giorah, one of the leaders, was brought captive to Rome, and died there as a gladiator. Johanan of Gishkala, another leader, was also dealt with severely by the Romans.

THE BOETHUSIANS (from originator—Boethus) were composed of the wealthy Pro-Roman politicians.

The Boethusians advocated complete submission to Rome. Josephus, one of their leaders, was made the Commander of the Northern front, the gateway to Jerusalem. He treacherously left the approaches to Jerusalem open. He was rewarded and honored by the Romans.

THE RABBINICAL AND KARAITE MOVEMENTS (*8th-10th Centuries C.E., which means Common Era.*)

During the period of the Gaonim the Jews were split by two factions, the Rabbinites and the Karaites.

The Rabbinites advocated observance not only of the laws of the Torah, but also of the laws passed by the Sages of the Talmua. The Karaites (organized by Anan ben David, 8th Century, C.E.), advocated strict observance of the laws of the Torah without the interpretations of the Sages. The Rabbinites won and excluded the Karaites from the Jewish community.

THE KABBALAH MOVEMENT (*15th Century C.E.*)

The Kabbalah movement advocated soul purification through good deeds, concentrated study of Torah, ethics, piety and fasting.

The Kabbalah originators were Rabbi Joseph Karo, author of the Shulchan Aruch, Rabbi Cordovero, and Rabbi Isaac Luria, called the Ari. Rabbi Vital, the pupil of Luria, spread the mystic idea of Kabbalism throughout Europe, by the use of the Zohar (the Kabbalistic book, said to be written by Rabbi Simon Bar Yochai [2nd Century C.E.], and published by the famous Mystic and scientist, De-Leon.)

SABBATANISM

(*See* Sabbatai Zvi in Section on Sages and Leaders, 17th Century.)

FRANKISM (*1759 C.E.*)

Frankism was organized by Jacob Frank, who claimed to be the reincarnation of Sabbatai Zvi. Jacob Frank and his followers ended by becoming Catholics.

HASIDISM (*18th Century C.E.*)

The Hasidic movement is based on the belief that simple worship is most acceptable to God. Prayers should come from the heart. People should approach God with joy and happiness and song.

The chief exponents of Hasidim were Rabbi Israel Baal Shem Tov called the Besht (as an abbreviation of Baal Shem

Tov), who originated the Hasidic idea (18th Century), and his follower, Rabbi Shneur Zalman, who made Hasidism a great part of Jewish life all over the world. The exponents of Hasidism claimed that numbers of Jews who are not scholars would like to serve God, and Hasidism gives them that opportunity.

Opposed to them were the Misnagdim (Opponents), whose chief was the Gaon (genius) Elijiah of Vilna, Lithuania (18th Century).

The Misnagdim claimed:

1. The Sages, beginning with Moses, always demanded detailed study of the Torah. Only an educated person can, by knowing and understanding the laws, be a truly pious Jew.
2. Hasidism tolerates ignorance. Only the Torah and Talmud keep the Jews united and strong.
3. Worshiping Hasidic Rabbis as miracle men, is against the Jewish idea of equality among people.

The Hasidim, on the other hand, claimed:

1. Hasidism would unite all Jews and strengthen their unity in the simple service and belief in God. Though the participants may not know the meanings of the prayers and the words, they may interpret them personally, be psychologically relieved and helped.
2. The belief in Hasidic Rabbis (the Tzadikim, or the pious) would relieve tension among Jews. The Hasidim look upon their Rabbis as the intermediaries of God, who make God more tangible to the people. The Hasidim could rely upon their Rabbis for advice and

help. It is not contrary to tradition to believe in Tzadikim as God's intermediaries, because the Prophets also acted as intermediaries of God. In ancient days the Jews relied upon the advice and help of the Prophets. The Tzadikim would fill the same need. The Hasidic Rabbis preached that simplification of one's problems leads to complete relaxation.

The Rabbis, by applying the essential psychology of Hasidism—namely, to let one talk freely in order to unburden oneself, whether through prayer to God or through talk with the Rabbi—achieved miraculous results. They were, therefore, venerated as great men by their followers. This idea might very well have influenced modern psychologists.

There are now some differences in the prayers used by the two groups. Each group claims to have the majority of Jews on its side.

HASKALAH MOVEMENT (*Enlightenment; 18th, 19th and 20th Centuries*)

The Haskalah movement flourished in the 18th and 19th Centuries. The Maskilim, or Enlighteners, advocated secular education among Jews in a Jewish national spirit, rather than having the Jews confine themselves to religious studies. They favored the use of the Hebrew language not only as a language of prayer, but also for daily use.

THE MUSAR MOVEMENT (*19th Century*)

The Musar movement advocates the supremacy of the Ethics of the Torah and the Talmud. It was founded by the Lithuanian Rabbi Israel Lipkin, called the Salanter, after the town of Salant, where he was the Rabbi. Based upon the Torah and the Talmud, these ethics stipulated that one should think good and practice good.

There are many folk stories told about the great Rabbi Israel Salanter; here are two of them:

Once, on the eve of Yom Kippur, the whole congregation waited for Rabbi Israel Salanter to arrive to chant the Kol Nidre. It was getting late and the people became concerned that something had happened to their great Rabbi. The messengers sent to fetch him did not find him at home. It seemed that he had disappeared. Finally, Rabbi Israel appeared in the synagogue. When the worried congregation asked him what had happened, he told them that on his way he heard a little child crying. The mother had left him sleeping and hurried to the synagogue for the Kol Nidre chanting. The Rabbi considered the welfare of the child more important than the punctual chanting of the Kol Nidre and he stayed to sing the baby to sleep.

Another time, when a plague of cholera was at its peak, the doctors cautioned no one to fast on Yom Kippur. When the people protested, Rabbi Israel stopped praying in the synagogue and began to eat, to set an example for the people. The members of the congregation followed their greatly revered Rabbi's example.

THE CHOFETZ CHAIM IDEA (*19th and 20th Centuries*)

Rabbi Israel Meyer Hakohen advocated the idea that one should refrain from deriding and criticizing others, and should first criticize himself. Derision of others is known in Hebrew as Lashon Horah.

Rabbi Meyer was revered by hundreds of thousands of people as a Tzadik (very pious man). He was of slight build, weighing only ninety-four pounds and curiously enough, he lived to the age of ninety-four. Slight as he was physically, he was a giant spiritually, with an exceptional will power. He wrote many books, which sold widely, in which he expounded his idea of refraining from Lashon Horah. His most famous book was the *Chofetz Chaim,* which means: "If you wish to live, guard your tongue from evil." Known throughout Jewry as the "Chofetz Chaim," Rabbi Meyer advocated silence as a treatment against Lashon Horah, believing that the less a person talks, the less Lashon Horah he will utter.

Zionism and Its Different Political and Ideological Movements (*19th and 20th Centuries*)

The most dynamic and modern Jewish movement is Zionism. This ideology advocates the return of the Jews to their ancient homeland and their existence there as an independent nation. The theory of political Zionism was established by Dr. Theodore Herzl after his study of the Dreyfus affair in France. Rabbi Zvi Hirsh Kalisher is considered to be the father of Spiritual Zionism.

POLITICAL ZIONISM

Captain Alfred Dreyfus, a Jew in the French army, was charged with having sold military secrets to the Germans. As was finally proved, his accusers were the actual traitors. The fight for Dreyfus was led by the famous French writer, Emil Zola, who charged the French General Staff with complicity in anti-Semitism.

Theodore Herzl (1860-1904), was an assimilated Jewish

journalist who had been assigned to cover the trial by a Viennese newspaper. Shocked by the scandals uncovered in the court, he came to the conclusion that only in their own land would the Jews be safe. No matter what privileges were accorded them in other countries, they would always be considered as strangers. To insure their security, he believed, the Jews must have their own state and government.

Herzl created the Zionist Organization, whose program was to create a state in the land of Israel. His efforts finally bore fruit in 1948, on May 14th, when the community in Israel set up a Government and declared its independence. It became a member of the United Nations in 1949.

Among those who helped evolve Herzl's theory of political Zionism were:

Max Nordau, Physician and sociologist, born in Hungary.
David Wolfson, French merchant.
Israel Zangwill, English writer.
Dr. Chaim Weizmann, scientist and first president of the State of Israel.
Nahum Sokolow, theoretician of Zionism and publicist.
Justice Louis D. Brandeis, American jurist.
Dr. Y. Tzlenoff, Russian leader.
M. M. Usishkin, Russian leader.

SPIRITUAL ZIONISM

Rabbi Zvi Hirsh Kalisher was the father of Spiritual Zionism. In 1862 he wrote his first article advocating rebuilding of Israel, in which God would help the Jews. This, according to Kalisher, does not conflict with the idea of the coming of the Messiah. (Up to this time the Jews had believed that they would return to Israel only when the Messiah came to lead them there). Rabbi Kalisher organized the Choveve Zion (Lovers of Zion) movement. Among its members were men of action who went to Palestine to settle there as pioneers (Halutzim). They called themselves "Bilu," an abbreviation of their slogan: "Beth Yaakov Lech V'Neilcha," which means "House of Jacob, let us go" (1878). Adolph Cremieux, French statesman, Montefiore the philanthropist and Rothschild, financed Rabbi Kalisher's ideas. They helped build the first modern Jewish colony in Palestine in 1869, which was called Mikve Israel (the gathering of Israel).

Dr. Leon Pinsker (1882), advocated the idea of Auto-Emancipation (self-emancipation) and published a book with that title. He held that the Jews must first free themselves from the idea of living in exile and begin to think in terms of living in an independent state. Once they had acquired that mental attitude, they would be able to translate it into action.

Moses Hess (1812-1875), was a famous Jewish leader who, even before Rabbi Kalisher and Dr. Pinsker, advocated the idea of self-determination of the Jewish people.

FIRST ZIONIST CONGRESS

Dr. Theodore Herzl called the First Zionist Congress in 1897 at Basle, Switzerland. Delegates came from all over the world. It seemed that the work of Jewish Sages who had advocated daily mention of Zion in prayers, and the work of the leaders of Spiritual Zionism, had finally brought results. The Congress accomplished the following:

1. A political organization known as the Zionist Organization was set up.
2. The annual dues would be one shekel.
3. The Zionist flag would consist of a white background

28

(symbol of peace), with two blue stripes (symbol of hope), and a Mogen David (shield of David, symbol of Israel's greatest era). This was proposed by David Wolfson. (The Zionist flag was copied from the Talith.)

4. Each member would work for the establishment of a publicly recognized and legally secured home for the Jewish people in the land of Israel.

5. The Jewish National Fund, organized by Herman Shapiro, was to collect money for the purchase of land in Israel. This would be the property of the Jewish people as a whole, belonging to no particular individual. The ablest administrators of the Fund were M. M. Usishkin and his American counterpart, Dr. Israel Goldstein, one of the leading Jews in present-day United States.

6. A National Bank was established.

After the First Zionist Congress, Herzl went to see the Sultan of Turkey, then ruler of Palestine, and Kaiser Wilhelm of Germany, a friend of the Sultan. He sought permission to establish a Jewish commonwealth in Palestine. But Kaiser Wilhelm, for political and personal reasons, did not favor the idea. England then offered Uganda in Africa as a temporary home for the Jews, but the majority of the Jews rejected it. In the midst of the controversy, Dr. Herzl died, July 3d, 1904.

CONCEPTS OF ZIONISM

Among the different approaches to both political and spiritual Zionism were:

29

ACHAD HA'AMISM

This movement was named after the writer Asher Ginsberg, who used the pen name of Achad Ha'am (one of the people). He advocated the establishment of a cultural and religious center in Palestine, rather than the establishment of a Jewish government. This idea was recently advocated by the late Dr. Judah Magnes, president of the Hebrew University, who also proposed a bi-national state in Palestine, composed of Arabs and Jews.

THE MIZRACHI MOVEMENT

Organized by Rabbi Reines who advocated a state of Israel based upon the precepts of the Torah.

THE LABOR ZIONIST MOVEMENTS

The various Labor Zionist Movements, organized by Dr. N. Syrkin, David Ben Gurion, Beer Boruchov and others, envisioned a state as based upon one or another of several socialistic theories. The first prime minister of Israel, David Ben Gurion is a member of the Socialistic Poale Zion (workers of Zion) movement, which goes under the name of Mapai in Israel. The Tzeire Zion (Young Zionists) movement was organized by Dr. Arlazarof.

THE REVISIONIST MOVEMENT

Organized by Vladimir Jabotinsky, foremost fighter, writer, speaker and organizer of the Jewish Legion in World War I. He advocated territories for Israel on both sides of the Jordan.

HADASSAH

A women's organization, founded by the American social worker, Henrietta Szold. It concerns itself, primarily, with the social and medical needs of the Jews in Israel. This organization built the famous Hadassah hospital and a number of other medical institutions throughout the country. It is also known for its social and educational programs for its members.

MAJOR POLITICAL PARTIES IN ISRAEL AT PRESENT

The Mapai, Mapam, and Achdut Avoda form the MA'ARACH (or Labor) BLOC.

The Herut, liberals, and religious bloc form the LIKUD BLOC.

None of the above have a majority in the Knesset and therefore have to depend upon religious parties such as the Mizrachi and Agudat Israel in order to have a voting majority.

There are also some splinter parties such as the Tehiyah, Arab parties, and the Communist party, which usually votes against any government.

TERRITORIALISM

Led by Israel Zangwill, it was organized when Herzl failed in his attempts to get the Sultan of Turkey, then ruler of Palestine, to permit Jews to establish a state there. The Territorialist party advocated the establishment of a Jewish homeland in Uganda, Africa, which had been offered for that purpose by England. Only a small number of Jews favored this plan.

THE BUND

The Bund, also known as the Jewish Socialist Workers' Party, was active in Russia, Poland and Lithuania at the beginning of the 20th Century. There were two movements in the Bund. One, led by Vladimir Medem, advocated a life in Diaspora, based upon a general socialist ideology. The other movement, led by Dr. Chaim Zitlovsky, advocated a Jewish life in the Diaspora based upon Jewish national life with the Yiddish language as the basis. The Bund opposed the Zionist movement on the grounds that since, under Socialism, there would be no Jewish problems, there was no need for a separate Jewish homeland. However, in view of historical developments in the past twenty years, there are indications of a friendlier and more understanding attitude on part of the Bund towards Israel in particular, and Jewish traditions in general.

NEO-ORTHODOXY (*19th Century*)

Expounded by Samson Raphael Hirsh, advocated strict observance of customs without the slightest changes.

CONSERVATISM (*19th Century*)

Expounded by Zahariah Frankel, advocated Judaism as a living spirit, which would undergo changes coming by themselves.

REFORMISM (*19th Century*)

Expounded by Abraham Geiger, advocated a conscious modification of traditional customs instead of waiting for changes to come by themselves.

RECONSTRUCTIONISM (*20th Century*)

A wing of the Conservative movement, originated by Dr. Mordecai Kaplan, which advocates a reconstruction of Jewish rituals and prayers.

CHAPTER TWO

JEWISH PROPHETS, SAGES
AND LEADERS

In our discussion of the history of the great people, we mentioned the names of the leaders who played so important a role in that history. In this chapter we will discuss the main points surrounding their careers and present some of the social reasons for their actions. We have omitted some of the leaders who are discussed in other chapters.

ABRAHAM

Hanoch and Noah believed in one God. But Abraham was the first to spread the belief in one God.

ISAAC

When visiting angels told Abraham that his wife, Sarah, would bear a son, she laughed, because Abraham was one hundred years old and she was ninety. The prophecy came true, and Abraham named his son Yitzchak (Isaac), from the Hebrew "Tzachok"—to laugh.

JACOB

Isaac had two sons, Esau the hunter and Jacob the shepherd. The Bible tells how Esau, returning famished from the hunt, came upon his brother Jacob cooking lentil soup. He offered his birthright in exchange for a plate of that soup. Birthright, in those times, carried many privileges. With it went the right to become master of the household and of all property, upon the death of the father.

When the aged Isaac wished to confirm Esau's birthright by blessing him, Rebecca, his wife, knowing about the sons' transaction, managed to substitute Jacob for Esau. Discovering the substitution, and realizing his loss, Esau sought to kill his brother. Jacob was forced to flee to his uncle Laban in Mesopotamia. There he met and fell in love with Laban's daughter, Rachel. In order to marry his beautiful cousin, Jacob agreed to work for her father for seven years. Upon completion of the set time, he found he had been tricked by Laban. Leah, another daughter, had been substituted for Rachel. Jacob, undeterred, served still another seven years in order to gain the hand of his chosen love.

JOSEPH

Joseph, the eleventh son of Jacob (the others sons of Jacob were: Reuben, Simon, Judah, Levi, Dan, Naphtali, Gad, Asher, Issachar, Zebulun, Benjamin and one daughter—Dinah), was sold into slavery by his brothers who resented the fact that he was Jacob's favorite.

He was bought by Potiphar, a wealthy officer of the Egyptian king, Pharaoh. Later, on a false charge by Zuleika, Potiphar's wife, Joseph was sent to prison. During his imprisonment, Egypt's Pharaoh had two strange dreams. When his seers failed to interpret them, the chief butler advised Pharaoh to call Joseph, who had once correctly interpreted a dream for him. The king related his dreams to the youth: "Seven lean cows consumed seven fat cows; seven lean ears of corn consumed seven full ears." The young Hebrew warned the king that this meant seven years of famine were coming, and that Egypt must prepare or be devastated. Impressed by his vision and wisdom, Pharaoh placed Joseph in charge of the nation's economy, with powers second only to his own. Later, Joseph married Osnath, who, according to interpreters, was the daughter of Potiphar.

Later, Joseph forgave his brothers and Jacob and his sons and their families settled in the province of Goshen, in Egypt.

MOSES (*13th Century B.C.E.*)

Moses was the son of Amram the Levite and Yocheved who, according to commentators, was a nurse by the professional name of Shifra. He was a brother of Aaron the high priest and of Miriam the prophetess who, according to commentators, was also a nurse like her mother. Her professional name was Puah.

Moses led the Jews out of Egypt where they were enslaved, and served as their leader in the desert on their way to Canaan, the Promised Land. He received the Torah directly from God, which to this day is the basis of Jewish law.

When Moses fled from Pharaoh, after killing a tyrannical Egyptian overseer, he went to the land of Midian. There he met the daughters of Jethro. When they brought him home, the girls introduced Moses as an Egyptian. He did not correct them by saying he was a Jew. Tradition tells us that, as a punishment for not protesting and not identifying himself immediately as a Jew, God did not permit Moses to enter the land of Israel.

According to another tradition, this punishment was imposed for a different reason. When the Jews were in the

35

desert and in great need of water, God instructed Moses to speak to a particular rock and water would come forth. Moses, however, in his impatience, struck the rock with his cane instead of talking to it. Because he set a bad example to the Jews by not following the exact instructions of God, he was not permitted to enter the land of Israel.

Aaron did not enter the promised land either, because he was with his brother, Moses, at that time and did not restrain him. However, before invading Canaan, Moses led the Jews in the battles, which won for them the lands across the Jordan.

JETHRO (*13th Century B.C.E.*)

Jethro served as chief adviser to Moses, whom he had saved from death in his infancy. While staying with Jethro, before returning to Egypt, Moses married Jethro's youngest daughter, Ziporah.

JOSHUA, CONQUEROR OF CANAAN (*13th Century, B.C.E.*)

Joshua (son of Nun), Moses' chief assistant and military leader, was appointed by Moses to succeed him. Kaleb, the son of Yefuneh and chief of tribe of Judah, was appointed as assistant to Joshua. They were fearless warriors and achieved the conquest of the land of Canaan.

Joshua and Kaleb were two of the original twelve who, forty years earlier had been sent by Moses to investigate secretly the situation in Canaan. They submitted to Moses a report recommending immediate attack. However, since the majority report advising delay had the support of most of the Jews, God punished them, by imposing upon them forty years of wandering in the desert—one year for each day the group had spent spying in Canaan.

The first city to be conquered was Jericho. Joshua sent Kaleb and Phineas, son of Eliezer, the high priest, to spy on the city. They brought a report advising an attack. Joshua had little trouble in conquering Jericho. Then came the city of Ai. Gradually the major part of Canaan was taken. Some sections, however, were occupied by different nations who later, after the tribes separated, successfully harassed the Jews.

The land was divided among the tribes in the following manner: Two and a half tribes received allotments in Trans-Jordan during the lifetime of Moses. The rest of the land was divided among the remainder of the tribes with the exception of the tribe of Levi. The Levites, not being farmers, but educators, assistants to the priests and administrators of the six cities of refuge, received no land but carried on with their own work.

JUDGES (*11th and 12th Centuries B.C.E.*)

After Joshua died, there was no one to take his place. Each tribe wanted its own head to become the common leader. The tribes separated and governed themselves independently. A state of anarchy prevailed in the land of Israel. (As written in the book of Judges: "Every man did as he pleased.") Little by little the neighboring, unfriendly nations gained control over the separated tribes. Sometimes a few tribes united, for a short time, to expel the invader; but they separated again. This condition lasted until the prophet Samuel became Judge. He reunited the Israelites.

The best known Judges were:

OTHNIEL, son-in-law of Kaleb, chief assistant to Joshua. He defeated the Arameans.

EHUD, who defeated the Moabites.

37

DEBORAH, the prophetess, who defeated the Canaanites with the help of her military commander, General Barak.

JEPHTACH, who defeated the Amonites. In fulfillment of a vow, he sacrificed his only daughter after the victory.

GIDEON, who defeated the Midianites. (His other name was Yerubaal, meaning, he who fought the idol, Baal.)

SAMSON, who defeated the Philistines, but, falling in love with a treacherous Philistine woman, Delilah, was captured by the enemy and blinded. (He had revealed to her the secret that his strength lay in his long hair; by cutting off his hair, Delilah caused Samson to lose his strength.)

(ABSALOM was another figure in Jewish history who lost his life on account of his long hair. The son of King David, Absalom rebelled against his father, but was finally defeated, though he had practically the whole Israeli army with him. In his attempt to escape, Absalom was caught by his hair in the branches of a tree and he was killed by David's General Joab, who was pursuing him.)

ELI, the high priest, who was defeated by the Philistines. He died of a fractured skull, after being told that his two sons were killed in battle and the Holy Ark was captured.

SAMUEL, who was Judge and Prophet. Against his will, when he became too old to continue ruling, he was forced to choose a king for the Israelites. He chose Saul, the farmer.

KING SAUL *(11th Century B.C.E.)*

Just as Samuel was unwilling to choose a king, so Saul, when chosen by Samuel, was unwilling to be king. He hid when he was so proclaimed. Later on however, when Saul had felt the taste of power, he was ready to kill David when he suspected him of being too popular with the people.

KING DAVID *(11th and 10th Century B.C.E.)*

King David was a great warrior and a great poet. He became a hero of the people as a child, when he slew the Philistine giant, Goliath. David's son, Solomon, was a great king and poet like himself. Both father and son wrote most of the Psalms, which to this day are chanted and quoted by people of many faiths.

King David's accomplishments:

1. Defeated the enemies of Israel.
2. Enlarged his kingdom to four times its original size.
3. United all the tribes into one strong nation.
4. Established Jerusalem as the Capitol of Israel.

KING SOLOMON *(10th Century B.C.E.)*

King Solomon's fame was widespread, and his accomplishments numerous:

1. Kept his country out of war for forty years. (His name Shlomoh—in Hebrew means peace.)
2. Built the Temple in Jerusalem *(960 B.C.E.)*, thus strengthening the spiritual ties among Jews.
3. Built a large merchant marine and carried on trade with many countries, even reaching South America according to some beliefs.
4. Organized a strong army, discouraging his neighbors from attacking Israel.

5. Built many beautiful edifices in the cities, roads, and a reservoir system still in operation.
6. Developed the country agriculturally by introducing artificial irrigation.
7. Developed smelting furnaces near the Gulf of Akaba.
8. Built cisterns of water for Jerusalem, a city previously indefensible because of lack of water.
9. Wrote many Psalms, the Song of Songs, Book of Proverbs, etc.
10. Became known as one of the wisest of men; but over-taxation caused protest among the people.

REHOBOAM AND JEROBOAM (930 B.C.E.)

After the death of Solomon, his son Rehoboam succeeded him. The people came to Rehoboam and asked him to ease the tax burden. Instead of quieting them, he told them he would impose heavier taxes.

Ten tribes, then under the leadership of Jeroboam, who for a long time had advocated secession, revolted and formed a separate kingdom of Israel, with Jeroboam as king. At first Jeroboam appeared to be a good king. Fearing, however, that in traveling to Jerusalem to serve God in the Temple, his people might reunite with Judea, he introduced idolatry into his kingdom. Thus, in keeping his subjects away from Jerusalem, he abandoned the principles of Judaism.

HOSEA, THE LAST KING OF ISRAEL (722 B.C.E.)

The last King of Israel was Hosea. He was defeated by Assyria and the Jews of Israel were exiled to distant lands and are lost without trace to this day.

ZEDEKIAH, THE LAST KING OF JUDEA (*586 B.C.E.*)

Judea's last king was Zedekiah, who revolted against Babylon. The revolt failed and Zedekiah and his sons were captured. Nebuchadnezzar, king of Babylon, blinded Zedekiah, killed his sons, destroyed the Temple and exiled the Jewish leaders and army officers to Babylon.

THE BEST KNOWN PROPHETS OF ISRAEL AND JUDEA

SAMUEL (*11th Century B.C.E.*), who was both prophet and the last of the Judges.

NATHAN (*11th Century B.C.E.*), who became famous through his scolding of King David for marrying Bathsheba, another man's wife.

ELIJAH (*9th Century B.C.E.*), has always been the most beloved prophet among Jews of all generations. He is renowned for his courage in fighting against idolatry, against the false prophets and priests of that time, and against Queen Jezebel, wife of King Ahab of Israel. Tradition holds that Elijah did not die, but ascended to heaven in a chariot of fire; that he will come back to announce the coming of the Messiah when peace will reign all over the world. There are hundreds of legends about Elijah. All unsolved questions on the Talmud end with the word *TEKU*, an abbreviation meaning "Elijah the Tishbite will clear this up in the future."

ELISHA (*9th Century B.C.E.*), his pupil, who succeeded him, was famous as a miracle healer. He resurrected the dead.

ISAIAH (*8th Century B.C.E.*), who preached during the reigns of the Judean kings, Uziah, Jotham, Ahaz and Hezekiah. Isaiah was not only a great prophet but a great statesman as well. It was he who advised the kings to remain neutral and to make no alliances with neighboring kingdoms. These he considered untrustworthy, labeling them, "The broken cane—not to be leaned upon."

To this day his sermons are quoted and read from pulpits of many faiths. As did other prophets, he denounced the oppression of the poor and the corruption of government officials. He preached God's vengeance not only against the Jewish oppressors but against the oppressors of other nations as well, who were then mighty and strong, but destined to perish by the hand of God. He is best known for preaching international peace. ("The wolf shall lie down with the lamb, the leopard with the sheep, nations shall beat their swords into ploughs and their spears into pruning hooks. But from Zion shall go forth the law of God and the word of the Lord shall come forth from Jerusalem.")

Isaiah preached against national and international violence. His voice seems to echo today in the halls of the United Nations, where modern-day prophets seek to build a peaceful world.

AMOS (*8th Century B.C.E.*), was the first prophet whose sermons were recorded. He is known for his denunciation of the rich for oppressing the poor.

JEREMIAH (*7th Century B.C.E.*), was one of the great prophets who witnessed the destruction of the first Temple.

Since the prophets served as the voice of public conscience, it is not surprising to find that Jeremiah preached against corruption in government. But in his sermons he also gave military and political counsel. It was Jeremiah's contention that Judea should postpone its battle against Babylon until a more propitious time, when God would take care of her. These sermons were misunderstood and King Zedekiah, who favored Egypt over Babylon, jailed him as a pro-Babylonian.

When Judea fell into the hands of the Babylonian king, Nebuchadnezzar, Jeremiah remained with the remnant of Jews to teach and advise them. After the murder of Gedaliah, the Jewish Governor appointed by the king of Babylon, he again followed his people into Egypt where he died a poor and broken man.

EZEKIEL (*6th Century B.C.E.*), was an international prophet. He preached and prophesied about most of the then known nations of his time. His sermon about Resurrection is best known as the sermon on the Dry Bones. The prophets among many others raised their voices against oppression. Their words were prophetic of freedom to come.

EZRA THE SCRIBE (*5th Century B.C.E.*)

When Cyrus, king of Persia, conquered Babylon, he issued a proclamation (537 B.C.E.) to the Jews to return to Judea and rebuild their land. There were three returns to Judea:

With Zerubabel in 538 B.C.E.
With Ezra in 457 B.C.E.
With Nehemiah in 455 B.C.E.

Ezra the Scribe, a pupil of Baruch, who was secretary to the prophet Jeremiah, settled in Judea with a few hundred Jews, who had responded to his call. There he discovered that most of the Jews had forgotten the Torah. In order to insure that this would never happen again, with the help of the Great Council or Assembly, which he organized, he instituted the weekly reading of a portion of the Torah and Prophets on each Saturday as well as on Holidays. This custom is still being observed in our time. With the help of the Great Assembly, which was composed of the most educated leaders of the community, he also arranged the Shmone Esrei or the Eighteen Prayers, said while standing. He simplified the Hebrew alphabet into the form used to this day.

He instituted many new laws and reforms among Jews. He and the members of his Council laid the foundation for the Talmud. Ezra, with the help of Nehemiah, a high official of the king of Persia, rebuilt the city of Jerusalem and the Temple.

ESTHER AND MORDECAI (450-350 B.C.E.)

These hundred years were called the Silent Century because little is known of what happened to the Jews during that period. They were then under the rule of Persia, which on the whole, appears to have been a tolerant rule. The one incident on record for that time, concerns the attempt of Haman, anti-Semitic prime-minister of King Ahasuerus, to exterminate the Jewish population of Persia. They were saved through the efforts of Mordecai, the leader of the Jews, and his cousin Esther, who was the wife of Ahasuerus. Haman was defeated and executed. The holiday of Purim is celebrated every year, to commemorate this event.

HOW THE NAME ALEXANDER ORIGINATED AMONG JEWS (4th Century B.C.E.)

This name originated among Jews from the name of Alexander the Great, king of Macedonia. When Alexander entered Jerusalem, the Jews gave him a friendly reception and won his friendship. When he wanted to put his statue in the Temple, as was the custom of the Greeks, the Jews could not agree. Instead they proposed to call every Jewish child born that year, by the name of Alexander, and to this he agreed. Since that time, Alexander has been a common Jewish name.

THE MACCABEAN WAR (*167-140 B.C.E.*)

The War of the Maccabees took place when the Jews were under the domination of the Greeks. Antiochus, the king, sought to Hellenize his Jewish subjects. This led to their revolt. Under the leadership of the Hasmonean brothers and their aged father Matathias, the revolt succeeded and an independent Jewish kingdom was established. The wars were called the Maccabean Wars, after the Jewish leader Judah the Maccabee (the Hammer).

HYRKAN, ARISTOBULUS AND ANTIPATER (*1st Century B.C.E.*)

After the death of the Hasmonean queen Shlomith Alexandra, Aristobulus, her younger son, seized the throne. He left his older brother Hyrkan in the post of high priest, which he held during his mother's reign.

Antipater, a converted Edomite, who was Hyrkan's adviser, counselled Hyrkan to seize the throne with the help of foreign troops from Arabia. Both brothers eventually turned to Pompey, the Roman governor of Syria, for help. Pompey favored Hyrkan because he was the weaker man, and appointed Antipater as his adviser. Aristobulus was arrested, and Judea became a province of Rome. Antipater was chosen governor.

45

HEROD AND CLEOPATRA (37-6 B.C.E.)

Because of his friendship with Cleopatra, Herod, Edomite son of Antipater, won from Rome the right to rule Judea. The Egyptian queen's influence over Caesar and Mark Anthony is well known. Through a tangled chain of influence then, Herod became ruler of Judea.

OCCUPATIONS OF THE SAGES

Many people believe that the ancient Sages were occupied only with study of the Torah and the Talmud. The fact is, however, that most of the hundreds of Talmudic Sages never received any remuneration from their study or teaching. Their study was their avocation. Their vocations, however, in many cases, involved physical hard work. The following are a few of the many:

Rabbi Joseph was a locksmith.
Rav Sheshet was a wood-carrier.
Simon, the Pakuli, was a wool-cleaner.
Jose, the son of Halaphta, was a tanner.
Rabbi Jose was a net-maker.
Rabbi Meir was a secretary and letter writer.
Rabbi Nehuniah was a ditch digger.
Rabbi Johanan was a shoemaker.
Abba Hoshiah was a launderer.
Rav Hisdah and *Rav Papa* were brewers.
Abba Bar Zeminah was a tailor.
Rav Adah Sabulah was a pearl-diver.
Rav Yehudah was a baker.
Hillel was a wood cutter, *Shammai,* a carpenter.
Rabbi Joshua, a blacksmith.

46

Rabbi Chanina, a shoemaker.

Rabbi Huna, a water-carrier.

Rabbi Simon Ben Lakish, called Resh-Lakish, was a circus performer.

HILLEL THE GREAT AND SHAMMAI (*1st Century B.C.E.*)

Hillel was the first to begin developing the Mishna as an exposition of the Torah. He also commented on decisions of former Sages, who were members of the Great Council. Hillel's contemporary was Shammai. Their pupils constituted, respectively, the House of Hillel and the House of Shammai, which often held diametrically opposed opinions on points of law. Shammai usually held to a strict interpretation of the law. Hillel's readings were more flexible. In the majority of cases Hillel's rulings prevailed and were followed by most of the scholars.

ONKLOS (*Acquila, 1st Century B.C.E.*)

Onklos, nephew of Emperor Nero, became a convert to Judaism and one of the greatest Jewish scholars of his time. He translated the Bible into Greek and then into Aramaic, spoken by the Jews at that time. This translation was so excellent that Rabbis decreed that, every Friday, pious Jews should read the weekly portion of the Torah twice in Hebrew and once in Onklos' Aramaic translation. This custom is still observed today.

RABBI JOHANAN BEN ZAKKAI (*70 C.E.*)

When the Romans under the command of General Vespasian were ready to conquer Jerusalem, since no one was allowed to leave the city, Rabbi Johanan was smuggled out in a coffin

47

by his pupils and brought before Vespasian. The Rabbi addressed Vespasian as "Your Majesty." At first Vespasian was angry because he was only a Roman general; just then news reached him that the Roman Senate had elected him Emperor. Impressed, he was ready to grant Rabbi Johanan anything he requested. Rabbi Johanan asked only for permission to organize a Yeshiva school of Talmudic study in the small town of Yavne. Vespasian readily granted what seemed to him such a small request. Rabbi Johanan fearing, however, the final extinction of the Jews as a nation, felt that a spiritual center in Yavne would sustain the Jews and keep alive their hope of regaining their national independence. History proved that Rabbi Johanan was right. Unwittingly Vespasian provided one of the keys to an independent nation.

RABBAN GAMALIEL (*1st Century C.E.*)

Rabban Gamaliel, chief of all the Jewish communities in his time, decreed that all Jewish funerals be conducted in a simple manner. This ruling was made to avoid embarrassment to the poor, keeping them from spending more than they could afford on elaborate funerals. It was and still is, therefore, mandatory that every Jew, regardless of how rich he may have been, be buried in simple linen and in a box made of plain boards—to denote that he came into the world with nothing and leaves it with nothing.

Rabban Gamaliel also arranged additions to the important Eighteen Prayers, called the Shmone Esrei or the Amida (standing while praying), said three times a day, every day in the year.

Rabban Gamaliel further contributed to the formation of

the Jewish Calendar in use today. The final arrangements were made by Hillel the Second in 360 C.E.

RABBI AKIBA, THE SHEPHERD (*2nd Century C.E.*)

The richest man in Judea, during the reigns of the Roman Emperors Hadrian and Trajan, was a man called Kalba Savua. His beautiful daughter Rachel, fell in love with one of his shepherds, Akiba, and secretly married him.

When Kalba Savua learned of this "disgrace," he discharged Akiba and disinherited Rachel.

For the love of his wife, Akiba went away to study and, by virtue of his outstanding talents, became one of the greatest of the Sages. Rabbi Akiba was the first compiler of the Mishna. Together he and his debating partner, Rabbi Ishmael devoted themselves to mysticism, a relatively new study. He also began compiling prayers for daily use.

As a shepherd, Rabbi Akiba had acquired a love for nature and freedom. He resolved to free Judea from the rule of Rome. He chose Bar Kochba, a man of high military qualities and a pupil of the Roman military school as military commander. Quietly, Bar Kochba raised and trained an army of over 400,000 men. Rebels of other nations joined them and a general revolt threatened Rome. Were it not for internal treachery, and a plague which broke out among Rabbi Akiba's pupils, leaders in the revolt, the might of Rome would have been broken. Although the revolt failed, Rabbi Akiba and Bar Kochba proved that Rome was not invincible.

From that time on, however, dark days fell upon the Jews. The Romans captured Rabbi Akiba and skinned him alive. They completely destroyed Jerusalem, drove the surviving

Jews into Exile, resettled the land with other people, and renamed it "Palestine" to indicate that the Jews had nothing to do with it. Only the extinct Philistines were considered natives.

RABBI MEIR AND BERURIA (*2nd Century C.E.*)

Rabbi Meir was one of the greatest of Talmudists of his time. Yet, highly respected as he was for his learning, his wife, Beruria, enjoyed even greater prestige as a result of her strength of character.

RAV (*3rd Century C.E.*)

The great Amorah Rav, of the famous debating team of Rav and Samuel was among the first of the Sages who advocated a return to farming for the Jews. He organized free lectures throughout the country of Babylon. They were so well attended that thousands of people slept in tents outside the cities in order to attend. He was the head of the Talmudic academy of Sura. Rav and Samuel were the interpreters of the Mishna, in Babylon.

SAMUEL THE ASTRONOMER (*3rd Century C.E.*)

Samuel was not only a great Talmudist but also a great doctor, mathematician and astronomer. He used to say that the lanes of heaven were as clear to him as the streets of Nahardea, the city where he was head of an academy. (Nahardea, Sura and Pombadita were the seats of the three great Jewish academies of learning.)

Samuel also decreed that the Jews should pray for the welfare of the government of the country in which they lived.

RAV HUNA AND RAV YEHUDA

Rav Huna and Rav Yehuda, successors to Rav and Samuel, were so sharp-witted and logical that it was said of them: "With their reasoning they can make an elephant pass through the eye of a needle."

ABBAIAH AND RABBAH, *founders of "Pilpul"* (*4th Century C.E.*)

"Pilpul" comes from the Hebrew Pilplin—meaning pepper. The symbol intended, is that the mind is as sharp as pepper. Pilpul has come to mean debate for the sake of debating, or "splitting hairs." It was a method of sharp argumentation used in the Talmudic Academies. It was based on the assumption that the earlier Sages were always right, therefore contradictions among them were only appearances and the underlying agreements could be arrived at by "Pilpul." But Abbaiah and Rabbah (who was called the mountain-shaker by his contemporaries, because he was considered to have the keenest mind of his generation), pupils of Rav Huna and Rav Yehudah, often argued not for the sake of finding a solution to a question, but to provide their pupils with mental exercise. In the 16th Century, Jacob Pollack reintroduced "Pilpul" in Europe.

SAADIA GAON (*10th Century C.E.*)

Saadia was the first grammarian. He simplified Hebrew grammar and translated the Torah and the Mishna into Arabic, thus introducing these great works into Arabic culture. In his "Emunoth V'deoth" he proves that the Jewish religion is based upon facts and reason.

Saadia Gaon won fame as the head of the chief Talmudic academy in Babylon, at the beginning of the Middle Ages. He fought the Karaites, a Jewish sect which advocated the literal observance of the Bible without Talmudic interpretation and succeeded in having them excommunicated. It was decreed: "A non-Jew may become a Jew, but never can a Karaite become a Jew."

THE GOLDEN ERA IN SPAIN (*900-1200 C.E.*)

When Spain came under the domination of the Moors, the Jews in that country entered what is known as their Golden Era. They occupied important positions in the government, in business, in science and in art. They developed and enriched their Hebrew culture to a remarkable degree. After the Christians conquered the Moors, the persecution of the Jews began again, and they were finally expelled from Spain by Ferdinand and Isabella in 1492.

Among the scholars and leaders of that time were:

MENAHEM BEN SARUK, secretary to the Vizier of Cordova, lexicographer and Bible commentator, who compiled a Hebrew dictionary.

DUNASH BEN LABRAT, poet, grammarian, first to distinguish between transitive and intransitive verbs.

JUDAH CHAYUJI, founder of the scientific study of grammar, wrote book on punctuation.

JOSEPH IBN MIGASH, commentator on the Talmud.

MOSES BEN CHANOCH, a Babylonian scholar, shipwrecked in Spain when it was under Moorish rule. He remained there and organized the Academy of Cordova, which became the educational center for Jews of Europe and Africa.

SAMUEL THE NAGID (The Prince), great scholar and gram·
marian, trusted adviser to the Caliph of Granada.

JOSEPH NAGID, son of Samuel the Nagid, who took his
father's place as adviser to the Caliph. He was killed
during anti-Semitic disturbances in Spain.

SAMUEL ABULAFIA, finance minister to King Pedro when
Aragon fell to the Christians.

JOSEPH ABARBANEL, also an adviser to King Pedro.

HASDAI IBN SHAPRUT, scholar and poet.

SOLOMON IBN GABIROL, a century after Ibn Shaprut, a
great poet and philosopher. Among his works are, *Mekor
Chaim* (*The Source of Life*) and *Kesser Malchut* (*The
Crown of the Ruler*). They are still read and quoted
today. His poems are chanted on Yom Kippur.

BAHYA IBN PAKUDA, writer and philosopher. His *Chovot
Halevovot* (*Duties of the Heart*), a book of ethics, continues to be read and studied.

RABBI ISAAC ALFASI, great Talmudic scholar, whose book
Halachot (*Laws*) was considered the final authority in
legal decisions of those days.

YEHUDAH HALEVI (*1080-1140*)

The greatest Jewish poet of all time. Jews still sing and
recite his songs of Zion. He was a great philosopher; his book
Kuzari, is still popular today. It consists of a three-sided
debate in which the disputants were a Jew, a Christian and
a Mohammedan. The debate was held at the court of Bulan,
king of the Kahzars, a Mongol nation which lived on the
Volga river in the eighth Century. The Kahzars became Jews.
Bulan was so impressed that he embraced Judaism.

While praying at the Wailing Wall (remnant of the

53

Temple) during a visit to Jerusalem, Halevi was killed by an Arab.

ABRAHAM IBN EZRA

Son-in-law of Halevi, Talmudist, mathematician, and linguist. He was materially poor but spiritually rich. Of his lack of material success, he said that were he a merchant of candles, the sun would never set; were he a merchant of shrouds, no one would ever die.

THE RAMBAM or MAIMONIDES (1135-1204 C.E.)

His name was Rabbi Moses ben Maimon, and Rambam is an abbreviation of that name. The Rambam was known as the greatest physician of his time, as well as the greatest philosopher, astronomer, mathematician and Talmudist. He was ranked with Moses the law giver. His best known works used to this day are:

MISHNE TORAH, a composition of fourteen volumes which simplifies the study of the Talmud.

PERUSH MISHNAYOTH, commentary on the Mishna, written in Arabic. A systematic arrangement of the Mishna which simplifies its study.

MOREI NEVUCHIM (*Guide to the Perplexed*), demonstrates the interrelation of religion and science. Maimonides asserted that there is no contradiction between the truth of the Torah and the truth of the human mind. Conflicts between religion and philosophy originated only because of misinterpretation of the Torah or of philosophy. In addition, he advanced important reasons to prove the existence of God. These were:

54

1. No motion can take place without an agent producing it.
2. There must be an agent which sets things in motion without itself being set in motion.
3. As there are things partially permanent and partially transient, there must be an agent who is permanently permanent.
4. Nothing could pass from potentiality into a state of actuality without the action of an agent.

Maimonides also sought to reconcile the Bible with the philosophy of Aristotle. He believed that every man, with sound physical, moral and mental faculties could become a prophet, and he discussed different forms of prophecy.

The final aim of the creation of the world, he asserted, is Man, and his happiness. To achieve happiness, man must exercise his intellect and must be beyond reproach, morally and intellectually. The intellect is to the soul what matter is to form, susceptible to both good and evil.

Maimonides enumerated man's obligations to himself and to his fellow men, as regards health through regular living. He called for:

1. Medical care when necessary.
2. Cleanliness.
3. Earning a livelihood.
4. Contentment of soul.
5. Moderation in joy and grief.
6. Kindness to animals.
7. Mutual love and sociability.
8. Respect for the property and honor of others.

According to Maimonides all these precepts are found in

the Torah. His thirteen Articles of Faith, to this day chanted every morning by Jews, are as follows:

1. God is our only leader.
2. God is one.
3. God has no body.
4. God is first and last.
5. We should pray to Him only.
6. The words of the Prophets are true.
7. The prophecies of Moses are true.
8. The Torah was given by God through Moses.
9. The Torah will never be changed.
10. God knows the thoughts of all.
11. God rewards good deeds and punishes evil.
12. We shall await the coming of Messiah.
13. We believe in the Resurrection of the dead.

THE RAMBAN

Also known as Moses ben Nachman, or Nachmanides, a contemporary of Maimonides. He was a Talmudist, physician, poet and polemicist.

BENJAMIN OF TUDELA

World traveler before Marco Polo. In his book, *Masaot Binyamin* (*Travels of Benjamin*), he describes his adventures and travels from Spain to the borders of China.

DON ISAAC ABARBANEL

Finance minister of Spain at the time the Jews were expelled. Although Isabella asked him to remain, Don Isaac refused and left with his people to settle in Italy. He was a Talmudist and philosopher.

RABEINU GERSHOM

He lived in Germany in the tenth century. He is best known as the Rabbi who decreed that:

1. A Jew may have no more than one wife.
2. A wife's consent must be obtained in a divorce.
3. Letters of others may not be tampered with.

Most Jews have accepted his recommendations.

RASHI (*1040-1105*)

Rashi, whose full name was Rabbi Shlomo Ytzhaki, wrote commentaries which are masterpieces of exposition. No Jew would venture to study Torah or Talmud without them. Rashi was a native of France.

THE TOSAFISTS (*12th Century C.E.*)

The Rashbam and Rabeinu Tam, grandsons of Rashi, both great Talmudists, made many important additional commentaries on the Talmud. Tosafist means "one who added."

RABBI SHAKNAH (*16th Century C.E.*)

Rabbi Shaknah organized the religious union of the three provinces of Polish Russia, Poland and Lithuania. This union was governed by a body of thirty men, with a layman as president. It collected taxes, organized schools for children, and directed all the internal affairs of the Jews under their jurisdiction.

JOSEPH MIGUES, DUKE OF NAXOS (*16th Century C.E.*)

Joseph Migues was a Marrano who escaped from Venice to

Turkey and became chief adviser to the Sultan. Through his political influence all over Europe, he was able to save many Jewish refugees. He sought to establish independent Jewish communities in Palestine, which was then under the rule of the Sultan. The response was weak, however, as the Jews then believed only the Messiah could bring them back to Palestine.

His mother-in-law, Doña Gracia Mendez, helped him considerably. She established the first Hebrew press in Turkey.

DAVID THE REUBENITE (*16th Century C.E.*)

In the 16th Century, there appeared in Europe a Jew who called himself David the Reubenite (David, from the tribe of Reuben). He claimed to have been sent by the ten lost tribes of Israel who had a powerful kingdom in Asia. David promised to save the Jews of Europe and Africa and reunite them with the ten tribes. For a while the Pope of Rome and the King of Portugal believed him. When it was discovered that no such kingdom of the lost tribes existed, the Portuguese King threw David the Reubenite, and Molcho, a high Portuguese official who, under David's influence had become a Jew, into prison.

SABBATAI ZVI, *the false Messiah* (*17th Century C.E.*)

The most notorious false Messiah was Sabbatai Zvi. He was a Turkish Jew who promised to bring all the Jews to Palestine by means of miracles. Becoming a nuisance to the Turkish Sultan, he was given the choice of embracing Mohammedanism or proving his claim to immortality by allowing himself to be shot at. When he chose conversion the movement began to deteriorate. Many oppressed European Jews, however, continued to believe in him, for Zvi promised an escape from their troubles.

MENASSEH BEN ISRAEL (*17th Century C.E.*)

Menasseh Ben Israel was a Jew from Holland. He went to England in 1652, upon the invitation of Oliver Cromwell, to discuss the readmission of Jews to England. (The Jews had been expelled in 1290.) He became one of Cromwell's ir timates.

BARUCH SPINOZA (*17th Century C.E.*)

Baruch Spinoza, by profession a lens-grinder, was considered the greatest philosopher of his time. He believed that:

1. God and nature are one.
2. Our existence follows laws of nature.
3. The most important thing in a human being is his mind.

MOSES MENDELSSOHN (*17th Century C.E.*)

In his attempt to encourage Jews to assimilate, Frederick the Great of Prussia had the help of his friend Moses Mendelssohn, philosopher and grandfather of the renowned composer, Felix Mendelssohn. Moses Mendelssohn believed that the Jews should observe not only their own customs, but also the customs of the Germans. He further held that they should study not only the Talmud, but also the literatures of other nations. As a result of his teachings, many young Jews left their religion to become full Germans and Christians. Mendelssohn's two daughters married Christians.

59

Jewish Friends of Queen Victoria of England

Besides Disraeli, Queen Victoria had other Jewish friends. Among them were:

MOSES MONTEFIORE, philanthropist and spokesman for his people. He was knighted by Queen Victoria. With Adolph Cremieux, a French statesman, he intervened in the Damascus affair, in which Jews of Syria were accused by monks of killing one of their members, in order to use his blood for Passover. The Jews were cleared of the charge.

LIONEL ROTHSCHILD, a member of Parliament and the head of the English branch of the Bank of Rothschild.

CHAPTER THREE

A BRIEF HISTORY OF THE JEWS IN VARIOUS COUNTRIES OF THE WORLD

The history of no country is complete without a consideration of the place of the Jews in that country. For the Jews have settled in all parts of the world. In this chapter we will trace briefly, the history of the Jews in many different countries, from their original settlement to the present time.

THE JEWS OF SPAIN

The first settlement of Jews in Spain came during Solomon's reign. With his Phoenician partner, King Hiram, Solomon sent ships to Spain and many Jews settled there. Others migrated to Spain when Israel came under the domination of Rome. When Spain was conquered by the Moors, the Jews rose to a position of eminence in the cultural, social, political and economic life of the country. But when the Moors were overthrown by the Christian rulers, Ferdinand and Isabella, the Jews were persecuted. The infamous Inquisition (1480 C.E.), a tribunal established in Spain to investigate the conduct of newly converted Catholics—demanded that the Jews either become Christians or leave the country. Most of these converted Catholics practised Judaism secretly and were called Marranos. The majority chose to leave, and in 1492 they were expelled from Spain. Before the Jews left, they vowed that they would never return to Spain. Only a handful ever returned.

THE JEWS OF PORTUGAL

The Jews in Portugal settled there at the same time as did their brothers in Spain, and were expelled during the same period (1497).

THE JEWS OF ITALY

The Jews first settled in Italy during the reign of Hyrkan, the Judean ruler, when the Romans signed a treaty of friendship with Judea. Jews were not molested in Italy until Paul IV became Pope. Paul IV forced the Jews to live in ghettos (restricted areas), and wear green badges to identify themselves.

This oppression came to an end in the 19th Century, when Napoleon conquered Italy. The Italian Jews were well treated from that time until the advent of Fascism under Mussolini. The persecution of the Italian Jews began in earnest when Mussolini became Hitler's junior Fascist partner. When Italian Fascism was overthrown in World War II, Italy became a Republic and the Jews regained full citizenship.

A famous Yeshiva was established in Italy during the Middle Ages at Padua. It was under the direction of Rabbi Judah Mintz.

THE JEWS OF TURKEY

When the Jews were expelled from Spain in 1492, Mohammed 2nd, conqueror of Constantinople, invited them to settle in the Turkish Empire. They settled, for the most part, in big cities, such as Saloniki, Smyrna, Alexandria and Cairo, and also in Palestine, then under Turkish rule. Except for minor incidents, they were treated as equal citizens.

Joseph, Duke of Naxos, a Marrano Jew from Spain, became the Sultan's adviser in the sixteenth century. He wanted to organize centralized Jewish life in Palestine and obtained the Sultan's consent. But the response of the Jews, however, was very weak. They believed that only the Messiah (deliverer) could lead them back to Israel. Many false Messiahs arose at that time, who made empty promises to the Jews and misled them. The most notorious of these was Sabbatai Zvi.

To this day Turkey has maintained a liberal policy toward the Jews. During the Hitler atrocities in Europe, many Jews found refuge there. Turkey was also the first Mohammedan country to recognize the State of Israel, and is on friendly terms with her.

THE JEWS OF HOLLAND

In the 1500's, during the reign of Charles V, who was also king of Spain and Portugal, the first Jews settled in Holland. The first to come were the Marranos, Lopez, Nunes and Tirado (1593 C.E.). Other Spanish and Portuguese Jews followed. One of the most prominent Jews of Holland was Manasseh Ben Israel (17th Century), a personal friend of Oliver Cromwell, Lord Protector of England.

The Jews were always treated well in Holland and had full rights as citizens. They established model schools, printing shops, great publishing houses. They developed the commerce of the country, particularly during the expansion of Holland as a colonial power.

The Jews of France

The Jews first came to France when Julius Caesar conquered Gaul. In the 11th, 12th and 13th Centuries the Jews of France suffered at the hands of the Crusaders. Pope Innocent III established the Inquisition in France, made Jews wear yellow badges, and forced them to live in ghettos. He also instigated the burning of the Talmud.

In the 14th Century the Jews were expelled from France and were not permitted to return until the 17th Century. During the French Revolution, the General Assembly proclaimed equal rights for all people, including Jews.

After the Napoleonic era, the Jews were treated as equal citizens and occupied high positions in the French government. Thus Leon Blum, René Myer and Pierre Mendez-France became Prime-Ministers of France. The French branch of the Rothschild banking house was famous all over the world. Only during the Dreyfus case and the brief period of collaboration with Hitler, after he conquered France, have the French Jews, in recent times, experienced difficulties. Now they are equal to other French citizens in all respects.

The Jews of Germany and Austria

During the same period that the Jews settled in France, they also settled in Germany. Up to the 11th Century they were not molested. With the start of the Crusades, however, they were greatly oppressed. In the 14th Century they were accused of causing the bubonic plague, found guilty by a court of public ignorance and superstition, and sentenced to mass murder. One of the greatest slaughters in history began. After the plague, the control of the country passed into the hands of barons, and each baron treated the Jews in his territory according to his will.

Martin Luther, in the early days of the Protestant Reformation, treated the Jews well, thinking they would join his Church. When he saw that they remained Jews, he began to attack them more violently than had the Catholics.

In Austria, which was a part of Germany, the majority of Jews lived in Vienna and were suppressed and oppressed there as in the rest of Germany. During the Thirty Years War they suffered from invasion and counter-invasion.

Emperor Joseph, in the 18th Century, issued an edict of toleration for the Jews. Frederick the Great of Prussia tried to induce the Jews to assimilate and become full Germans, and his friend, Moses Mendelssohn, aided him in this endeavor. Bismarck, a clever man, who understood the importance of the Jews in Germany, in the fields of industry and commerce, tolerated them.

The end of World War I found German Jews in high places, but the groundwork was being laid for the Hitler brand of anti-Semitism. Countless books and publications appeared on the market to discredit and undermine the Jews. A Jewish bogey-man, responsible for the ills of a sick nation, was being created. When the Nazis finally came to power, and the big lie of a super-race was swallowed by the German people, the Jew became a perfect scape-goat for despots.

Up to and including World War II, most of the Jews in Germany, Austria and the other European countries conquered by the Nazis, were herded into concentration and slave-labor camps. A ghastly program of extermination was put into practice, and over six million Jews were murdered.

When the Allies defeated Germany, they found little left of its Jewish population. Most of the remaining few abandoned the land of blood and suffering to build a new life in the State of Israel.

THE JEWS OF ENGLAND

The first Jews entered England during the reign of William the Conqueror. They were expelled from England in 1200 C.E., but returned during the reign of Oliver Cromwell. In 1865 the House of Commons granted citizenship to the Jews of England. Many Jews rose to power, among them Disraeli. He became one of the most renowned Prime Ministers, during the reign of Queen Victoria. Moses Montefiore (philanthropist), Montague (industrialist), and Rothschild (banker), achieved comparable prominence.

During the first World War, England, through her foreign minister, Lord Balfour, issued a declaration pledging to help establish a national home for the Jews in Palestine. England's first Palestinian High Commissioner was a Jew, Herbert Samuel. Nevertheless, he put obstacles in the way of the Jews. England separated Trans-Jordan from Palestine proper, and enacted laws restricting immigration and the purchase of land by Jews. Finally, in 1948, Jews succeeded in establishing an independent State of Israel. (See Addenda, p. 223.)

THE JEWS OF LITHUANIA

The first Jews to settle in Lithuania in the 11th Century came from the land of the Khazars, on the lower Volga River, from Crimea on the Black Sea and from Bohemia. Originally the Jews came to the land of the Khazars from the Byzantine kingdom, where they had been oppressed. The Khazars had welcomed the Jews and later had been converted to Judaism. When the Khazars were overrun by the Mongols and Russians, the Jews settled in Lithuania, whose rulers, at that time, were extremely tolerant.

Persecution began, however, when Jagello became the ruler of both Poland and Lithuania. Thereafter, under the influence of the Catholic clergy, the rulers harried the Jews. When Lithuania fell under the rule of Russia, during the reign of Catherine the Great, the Jews were treated as second-class citizens. They were allowed to live only in restricted sections, and they could not receive a secular education. Only a certain percentage of the youth could enter their schools. Most Jews were restricted in travel and commerce.

After the first World War, Lithuania became an independent republic. For a while, the Jews were treated well; but, later, oppression began again. During World War II, Lithuanians helped the Nazis kill Jews. After the war, Lithuania became part of the Soviet Union. There are few Jews left today, only about 4000 out of 200,000 before the war. Present-day restrictive immigration laws serve to prevent Jewish emigration from Lithuania.

THE JEWS OF RUSSIA

The first Jews to settle in Russia came from Persia, Armenia, and Byzantia in the first Century, and during the reign of the first Russian ruler, Rurik. When the Tartars invaded Russia, the Jewish population moved to the northern province of Russia, Novgorod. In the 15th Century a religious movement, called "the Jewish heresy," spread in Russia through the efforts of a Jew, named Zachariah. Many nobles and Christian priests became Jews.

To suppress the movement, all its leaders were killed, and all Jews banished from Russia. During the reign of Catherine the Great, Russia acquired Lithuania and Poland with their large Jewish populations. Catherine permitted Jews to travel through Russia but not to live there. During the reign of her grandson, Alexander I, Jews were forbidden to live in villages or work as farmers. During the reign of his brother, Nicholas I, small Jewish children were taken forcibly from their parents and trained to be soldiers for the rest of their lives.

The Jews of Russia were finally recognized as equal citizens after the Revolution in 1917. When the question of recognizing Israel as an independent state came before the United Nations, the United States and Russia were the first to advocate recognition. (See Addenda, p. 223.)

THE JEWS OF POLAND

The Polish Jews originally came from Germany, Austria and Bohemia in the 11th Century, at about the same time as the Jews came to Lithuania from the Volga section.

At first the Polish rulers treated the Jews very well, particuarly Boleslav and Kazimir the Great, who had a Jewish wife, Esther. When Jagello became king, oppression began. In the 17th Century there was a revolt of the Cossacks in the Ukraine, which then belonged to Poland. The Cossacks, incited by Russia, killed over 300,000 Jews. The Cossacks later united with Russia. Instead of uniting with the Jews against the Cossacks, the Poles helped the Cossacks kill the Jews. They were later killed themselves. During the reign of Catherine the Great, when Poland came under the domination of Russia, the Polish Jews shared the fate of the Lithuanian and Russian Jews. After the first World War, when Poland became an independent republic, the Jews were at first treated fairly well but, unfortunately, this period of fair treatment was short-lived. Poland became notorious, even before its conquest by Hitler, for the oppression of the Jews. This oppression became outright murder during Hitler's occupation of Poland when several million Polish Jews were exterminated. However, the Jews of Poland in the great "Warsaw Ghetto Uprising" against the Nazis wrote a heroic page in Jewish history.

THE JEWS OF NORTH AFRICA

The Jews settled in North Africa in the early days of the Roman Empire. They came from Judea and Rome. It is also believed that some Jews had settled there during the reign of Solomon. They spread down to the desert and became warlike tribes. After Spain was conquered by the Christians, the position of the Jews deteriorated in North Africa. They were restricted in Mellas (ghettos) and were greatly oppressed.

With the establishment of the State of Israel, thousands of Jews have been brought from this oppression in North Africa to freedom in Israel.

THE JEWS OF EGYPT

Jews have lived in Egypt since time immemorial. Solomon's favorite wife was the daughter of the Pharaoh. In the reign of the dynasty of the Ptolemies, Judea was under the rule of Egypt. In the days of the Romans, there were in Egypt over one million Jews. After the Arab conquest of Egypt, the Jews were treated well and occupied high positions in the government. Maimonides was physician to the Caliph. When the Turks occupied Egypt, the Jews received equal treatment with the Arabs. But when the State of Israel was established in 1948, Egypt became its chief opponent, and oppressed the

Jews within its own boundaries. In its war for independence, Israel defeated Egypt and signed an armistice, hoping that peaceful relations between the two countries would be established. Unfortunately, Egypt still displays hostility towards Israel. (See Addenda, p. 223.)

THE JEWS OF ETHIOPIA

A Jewish professor, Faitelowitch discovered a Jewish group called Falashas (strangers) in Ethiopia. Up to the 16th Century the Falashas, it seems, were in the majority and dominant. Later they were defeated and the population became predominantly Christian. The Falashas follow some precepts of the Torah but have nothing to do with Talmudic laws.

The Falashas were given spiritual help by European Jews, after they had been discovered by Faitelowitch. During the Mussolini invasion, help had to be suspended. With the return of Haile Selassie, it was resumed. Falashas are in contact with Israel and other Jewish communities. (See Addenda, p. 223.)

THE JEWS OF SOUTH AFRICA

Jews came to South Africa together with the Dutch and the English. In the 20th Century, most came in flight from pogroms in Russia. A large number of Lithuanian Jews settled there and prospered. They form the largest segment of Jewry of South Africa.

THE JEWS OF YEMEN

Yemen lies at the southern tip of the Arabian peninsula on the Red Sea, across Ethiopia. It is believed to be the ancient kingdom of Sheba. It is also believed that the first Jews came to Yemen in the days of Jeremiah the prophet. The Jews of

Yemen always kept in touch with the Jews of Israel and Babylonia. In 1677, an edict to expel the Jews was issued by the Arab authorities. However, it was later rescinded. But from that time, life for the Jews in Yemen became intolerable. Finally the greater part of those Jews migrated to Israel.

THE JEWS OF PERSIA (IRAN)

The Jews settled in Persia when Cyrus issued a proclamation restoring Jewish community life in Judea, in the days of Ezra and Nehemiah. When we study the background of Purim, which happened during the "Silent Century" (350-450 B.C.E.), the story indicates that the Jews were numerous and a powerful group in Persia. When the fire-worshippers ruled Persia, the Jews rebelled under the leadership of Mar-Zutra. They succeeded in gaining temporary independence for the section where the Jews lived, but the rebellion was crushed and ever since, the Jews in Persia have been oppressed. Most of them migrated to Palestine and neighboring countries, but a small number remain in Persia.

THE JEWS OF IRAQ, LEBANON, SYRIA, RUSSIAN GEORGIA, ARMENIA

Jews have lived in these countries from very early times. They came to Babylonia after the destruction of the first Temple. From there, they spread into Georgia and Armenia. Iraq now occupies part of what used to be Babylon. In Lebanon, Jews settled in the days of Solomon, who was a partner in many enterprises, of King Hiram, of ancient Phoenicia, the present Lebanon.

In 1948, Iraq, Lebanon and Syria combined against Israel, and were defeated. They signed an armistice, but have refused to make peace. Only time will tell, whether they will agree to a peaceful settlement with Israel. In the meantime, they oppress the Jews living in their countries. Israel has succeeded in receiving and settling most of the Jews from Iraq. They are attempting to help the remainder from Syria, Iraq and Lebanon.

The Jews in Georgia and Armenia, who have lived there for centuries, are believed by some to be part of the Ten Lost Tribes. They are mostly farmers. Some, together with Jews from Bukhara and Turkestan (also part of the Soviet Union), managed to migrate to Israel.

THE JEWS OF CHINA

It is believed that Jews settled in China during the days of Roman trade with that country. Chinese Jews are known to have existed then who worshipped in Synagogues, in which were found scrolls of the Torah, copies of the Prophets and other Jewish writings.

Jews were treated fairly well in China; but with the occupation by Japan, an ally of Hitler, Jews were persecuted. At present, under Communist rule, the Jews are treated as in Russia.

THE JEWS OF INDIA

It is believed that the first Jews who settled in India came before the destruction of the Second Temple. They came from Egypt and from Babylonia. Benjamin of Tudela, in his book *The Travels of Benjamin,* describes his meeting with Jews in India, many years before Marco Polo. European Jews settled many years later. Relations between the two groups are cordial. The Jews in India number about 25,000.

THE JEWS OF JAPAN

The first Jews to come to Japan were believed to come from China, in the second Century, C.E. Their number was very small and remained small because of the Japanese policy of isolation from Europeans up to the middle of the 19th Century. A number of Jews came to Japan from Russia after the Russian Revolution, but most migrated to other countries, principally the United States. During World War II, when Japan allied itself with Germany, its policy toward Jews took on a Nazi tinge. At present, the few Jews in Japan are mostly citizens of other countries.

THE JEWS IN THE PHILIPPINES AND OTHER PACIFIC ISLANDS

The first Jews came to the Pacific Islands when Spain conquered them. They came as Marranos. After World War I, a number of Russian Jews settled there. The largest number settled in Manila. In other Pacific Islands, Jews arrived with the Dutch.

THE JEWS OF SOUTH AMERICA

The first Jewish settlement in South America was in Recife, Brazil, during the occupation by the Dutch. Upon its reoccupation by the Portguese they had to flee from persecution by the Inquisition. Most of them were Marranos.

After the 19th Century, however, most countries of South America began to serve as a haven of refuge for oppressed Jews of Europe, until the number of Jews reached close to a million. The biggest Jewish communities are in Argentina and Brazil, where they have an active spiritual and communal life. Relations with the South American governments are good. Some of them are strong supporters of an independent State of Israel.

The Jews of Australia

The first Jews arrived in Australia in 1817, along with British colonists. They were mostly English and Polish Jews. In the late 19th Century, and after World War I, a new wave of Russian Jews entered Australia. There are at present about 75,000 Jews in Australia and New Zealand.

The Jews of Canada

It is believed that one of the first Viceroys of New France (1625), Henry DeLevy, was a Jew. It is remarkable that his coat of arms had three Stars of David.

In 1732, six French ships with Jews settled on the island of St. John, now Prince Edward Island.

In 1757, Abraham Gradis supplied ships to General Montcalm to fight against the British.

The first Jew to settle in Canada during the British occupation was Aaron Hart, who came to Canada in 1752.

Uriah Judah, Levy Solomons, Ezekiel Solomons, and Simon Levy were among the Jews who came to Montreal in 1760, as pioneers.

The first Jewish community Congregation was established in Montreal in 1768, and the first synagogue was built in Montreal in 1777.

During the American Revolutionary War, David Franks fought with the British, while David Salesby Franks and Col. Isaac Franks, Canadian Jews, fought with Washington.

In 1830, Jews were granted full civil rights in Canada.

The first Jewish society, "The Hebrew Philanthropic Society," was organized in Canada in 1847.

One of the best and first known Maskilim in Canada was the famous scholar Alexander Harkavi (1863-1939). He was a teacher, writer and organizer.

Canadian Jews organized in 1890 the Jewish Colonization Association.

In social life, Canadian Jews have close ties with the American Jewish organizations. Examples are, the Canadian Jewish Congress, the National Council of Jewish Women, the Zionist Organization, Hadassah, etc.

JEWISH POPULATION IN DIFFERENT COUNTRIES OF THE WORLD: 1982

EUROPE
Austria—13,000
Belgium—41,100
Bulgaria—7,000
Czechoslovakia—13,000
Denmark—7,500
Eire—5,400
Finland—13,200
France—650,000
Germany—34,000
Great Britain—420,000
Greece—6,000
Holland—30,000
Hungary—85,000
Italy—39,000
Norway—850
Poland—6,000
Rumania—34,500
Spain—10,000
Sweden—16,000
Switzerland—21,000
Soviet Union—2,180,000
Turkey—27,000
Yugoslavia—6,000

AUSTRALIA
Australia—70,000
New Zealand—5,000

ASIA
Afghanistan—100
China—300
India—8,000
Iraq—350
Israel—4,100,000
Japan—400
Lebanon—410
Philippines—200
Syria—4,300

AFRICA
Algeria—1,000
Egypt—21,000
Ethiopia—22,000
Libya—20
Morocco—18,000
Tunisia—7,000
Union of South Africa—
    118,000

NORTH A'MERICA
Canada—320,000
Cuba—1,200
Jamaica—500
Mexico—38,000
United States—6,100,000

SOUTH AMERICA
Argentine—300,000
Bolivia—2,000
Brazil—150,000
Chile—27,000
Columbia—12,000
Ecuador—1,000
Guatemala—2,000
Panama—2,100
Peru—5,200
Uruguay—50,000
Venezuela—15,000

Jewish Population of Israel: 1982—4,100,000

Acre—36,000
Afula—18,800
Ashdod—54,000
Ashkelon—49,000
Beer-Sheba—99,000
Dimona—28,000
Elath—11,700
Haifa—227,900
Herzlia—50,000
Hebron—45,000
Hedera—36,200
Jerusalem—366,000

Kfor Saba—33,800
Kiryat Shmone—16,000
Lod (or Lydda)—37,000
Naharia—27,500
Nazareth—57,000
Nathania—86,000
Ramleh—37,500
Rehobot—54,500
Rishon L'Tzion—73,500
Shechem—50,200
Tel Aviv—394,000
Tiberias—27,500

CHAPTER FOUR

AMERICAN JEWRY

Among the ancient Indians of the Western Hemisphere,
traces have been found of Jewish influence.

It has been asserted that in the days of King Solomon,
Jews visited and traded with the Indians of Peru. Certain
legends and customs of the Peruvian Indians lend some support to the belief that the land of Ofir, mentioned in the
prophets, was Peru.

JEWS WHO HELPED COLUMBUS IN THE DISCOVERY OF AMERICA

JUDAH CRESQUES, known as the map Jew. He supplied
Columbus with maps and charts.

JOSEPH VECHINTO, a court physician.

LOUIS ST. ANGEL, chancellor of the Spanish court. With
the active support of the king, he backed Columbus with
five million Maravedis (Spanish currency).

ABRAHAM ZACCUTO prepared astronomical tables for
Columbus.

RODERIGO SANCHEZ, Inspector General of the expedition.

BERNAL, chief medical officer of the expedition.

DE TRIANO, master sailor and a member of the expedition.

MARKO, surgeon.

LUIS DE TORRES, interpreter for Columbus. He was the

first to set foot in the new land, and the first to bring tobacco to Europe from the new world. He also introduced the turkey bird. "Turkey" comes from the Hebrew "Tukkey," which means an Indian rooster or parrot. Columbus thought he had landed in India. When de Torres, his interpreter, saw a turkey, he called it "tukkey," thinking it was an Indian bird.

All of these men were Marranos (secret Jews) as were other sailors on the expedition.

First Jewish Colony in the New World (*1620*)

The Jews settled in Brazil during the period when it was captured by the Dutch. They formed their first colony in Recife. When Brazil was reconquered by the Portuguese, the Jews moved to Surinam, Curaçao, Cayenne and Dutch Guiana in order to escape persecution.

In 1680 Samuel Nasi bought an island near Surinam and founded a Jewish colony there which he called Jewish Savannah. It was later destroyed during a revolt.

First Jews in New Amsterdam

In the first week of September, 1654, twenty-three Jews arrived in New Amsterdam, fleeing from Portuguese inquisition in Brazil. This event was celebrated throughout the United States in 1954, the year marking the Tercentenary of the first arrival of the Jews to this country.

The Jews established their first cemetery in 1655, in New Amsterdam, near what is now Chatham Square. They organized their first central congregation in New York in 1685. Their first synagogue was the Shearit Israel (Remnant of

Israel), on Mill Street, built in 1730. It still exists today as
the Spanish Portuguese Synagogue on Central Park West.

THE FIRST DEMAND FOR EQUAL RIGHTS IN NEW AMSTERDAM (*1655*)

Asher Levy demanded equal rights with the other burghers
to serve in the guard. Peter Stuyvesant, the governor of
New Amsterdam, who was unfriendly to Jews, refused to
grant the request. The question was brought before the stock-
holders of the West Indies Company in Holland, several of
whom were Jews. They decided that, since the Jews had
equal rights in Holland, they should be accorded the same
treatment in the colonies. Thereafter, the Jews of New
Amsterdam were recognized as full citizens.

EARLY JEWISH SETTLEMENTS IN THE UNITED STATES

The second Jewish settlement in the United States, following
the Jewish community in New Amsterdam, was at Newport,
Rhode Island. These settlers were attracted to Rhode Island
by the policy of religious freedom instituted by Roger Wil-
liams.

The Jews settled in Pennsylvania in 1726.

The first Jew to settle in Baltimore was Jacob Lumbrozo,
a physician, who arrived there in 1656.

The first Jews to arrive in Georgia, in 1733, were Portuguese Jews.

JEWS WHO WERE ACTIVE IN THE WAR FOR INDE-PENDENCE

There were nine Jews among the merchants who signed the
Non-Importation agreement of Philadelphia on October 25th,

1765. The signers agreed not to import goods from England until Great Britain abandoned the impositions on the Colonies.

FRANCIS SALVADOR of South Carolina was the first Jew to die in the American Revolution. He was killed in battle on August 1, 1776, less than a month after the Declaration of Independence was signed. Salvador was also the first Jew to hold state office in America, being elected a member of the first Provincial Congress of South Carolina in 1774.

COLONEL DAVID S. FRANKS and MORDECAI SHEFTEL played important military roles in the Revolutionary War.

GERSHOM MENDES SEIXAS was the Rabbi of the Shearit Israel Synagogue. When the British seized New York, he and his congregation refused to remain in the city. Rabbi Seixas followed his congregation to Philadelphia, where he worked unceasingly for the revolutionary cause.

HAYM SALOMON was a Polish Jew who raised funds for Washington's army during the most critical days of the Revolution. He also gave financial aid to members of the Continental Congress, among them James Madison. With his sizeable contributions, Salomon enabled many leaders of the Revolution to carry out their important work. He also displayed acts of personal valor by repeatedly riding through enemy lines carrying money and important information. Even when he was imprisoned by the British, he continued to carry on "intelligence" activity in the revolutionary cause. This he did by pretending to be serving the British as an interpreter.

On December 15, 1941, the debt due to Haym Salomon for his contributions to victory in the War for Independence was fully recognized. In Chicago on that day, the George Washington-Robert Morris-Haym Salomon monument was unveiled. In August, 1936, when the plan for such a monument was announced by the Patriotic Foundation of Chicago, President Franklin D. Roosevelt wrote: "It was never disputed that at a critical period in the affairs of the Revolution, Haym Salomon came to the rescue of the Continental Congress with loans freely extended. The debt of gratitude which the Nation owes Salomon's memory will in part be paid through the fulfillment of plans of the Patriotic Foundation to erect in Chicago a monument which will portray Salomon with his fellow patriots, George Washington and Robert Morris. I bespeak for the undertaking the fullest measure of success."

BENJAMIN NONES served under Generals Pulaski, Dekalb, Lafayette and Washington. He was one of many Jews who supported Thomas Jefferson and the Democratic-Republican movement which he led.

In 1800, the Federalist Party, through its semi-official organ, *The Gazette of the United States,* attacked Nones for the triple "crime" of being poor, a Jeffersonian, and a Jew. Nones' reply, rejected by the *Gazette,* was printed in the Philadelphia *Aurora,* leading newspaper of the Democratic-Republican Party of Jefferson, on August 11, 1800. Excerpts from this important document of American-Jewish history follow:

"I am accused of being a Jew; of being a Republican; and of being poor.

"I am a Jew. I glory in belonging to that persuasion.

"To be of such a persuasion, is to me no disgrace; though I well understand the inhuman language of bigoted contempt, in which your reporter, by attempting to make me ridiculous

81

as a Jew, has made himself detestable whatever religious persuasion may be dishonored by his adherence.

"I am a Jew, and if for no other reason, for that reason I am a Republican. In the monarchies of Europe, we are hunted from society—stigmatized as unworthy of common civility, thrust out as it were from the converse of men; objects of mockery and insult to froward children, the butts of vulgar wit, and low buffoonery. Among the nations of Europe we are inhabitants everywhere—but citizens nowhere—unless in Republics.

"How then can a Jew but be a Republican? In America particularly. Unfeeling and ungrateful would he be, if he were callous to the glorious and benevolent cause of the differences between his situation in this land of freedom and among the proud and privileged law givers of Europe.

"But I am poor, I am so, my family is also large, but soberly and decently brought up. They have not been taught to revile a Christian because his religion is not so old as theirs.

"The public will now judge who is the proper object of ridicule and contempt."

After the War for Independence, Washington personally wrote letters congratulating the Jewish community, and thanking them for their valuable help. Several Hebrew Congregations hailed the election of Washington as first President of the United States, and expressed their loyalty to the American Government. In his famous reply to the Jewish Congregation of Newport, George Washington emphasized the equality of all American citizens irrespective of creed:

"All possess alike liberty of conscience and immunities of citizenship. It is now no more that *toleration* is spoken of, as if it was by the indulgence of one class of people, that another enjoyed the exercise of their inherent natural rights. For, happily, the government of the United States which gives to bigotry no sanction, to persecution no assistance, requires only that they who live under its protection, should demean themselves as good citizens. . . .

"May the children of the stock of Abraham who dwell in this land, continue to merit and enjoy the good will of the other inhabitants; while everyone shall sit in safety under his own vine and fig-tree, and there shall be none to make him afraid."

JEWS IN THE CIVIL WAR

The majority of Jews sided with the North on the slavery issue, because Jews are traditionally opposed to slavery. There was, however, a minority which sided with the Confederates. Among those strongly supporting Lincoln were LEWIS DEMBITZ, uncle of Louis D. Brandeis, United States Supreme Court Justice; ABRAHAM KOHN, clerk of the city of Chicago and ABRAHAM JONES of Quincy, Illinois.

DAVID YULEE, first senator from Florida, and JUDAH P. BENJAMIN, were considered to be part of the ideological leadership of the Confederate Government.

Judah P. Benjamin was born of poor parents in 1811 in the British West Indies. His parents, Sephardic Jews, came to North Carolina when Judah was two years old. Nine years later the family moved to Charleston. After a turbulent career in Yale University, Benjamin settled in New Orleans in 1828 without money or friends. His rise to national eminence as a lawyer and businessman was phenomenal, and he soon became financially independent.

83

Benjamin was elected United States Senator from Louisiana in 1853, and was reelected in 1859. As a Senator, he gained national prominence for his speeches defending slavery and attacking the anti-slavery movement. During the Civil War he occupied the posts of Attorney-General, Secretary of War and Secretary of State for the Southern Confederacy. He has been frequently referred to by historians as "the brains of the Confederacy."

Two famous Rabbis who spoke out vigorously against slavery were The Reverend Dr. Bernard Felsenthal of Chicago and The Reverend Dr. David Einhorn of Baltimore. Addressing themselves to those Jews who defended slavery, Dr. Felsenthal wrote:

"People who have themselves experienced how on the European continent the feudalists and clerics argued that they belonged to an inferior race, that they would, when emancipated, deprive Christians of bread, that they are condemned to eternal slavery through divine ordinance, that they would overrun from everywhere that State which declared them complete citizens, etc., such people are narrow and vulgar enough to advance the same arguments against the emancipation of the Negroes! If anyone, it should be the Jew above all who ought to cultivate the most glowing and most irreconcilable hatred towards 'the peculiar institution of the South' and who ought to make his slogan: *fiat justico, pereat mundus*. (Justice, even though the world were to be destroyed.)"

Attacking those who argued that the Bible justified slavery, Dr. Einhorn wrote:

"Can *that* Book hallow the enslavement of any race, which sets out with the principles that Adam was created in the image of God, and that all men have descended from *one*

84

human pair? Can *that* Book mean to raise the whip and forge chains, which proclaims, with flaming words, in the name of God: 'Break the bonds of oppression, let the oppressed go free, and tear every yoke!" Can *that* Book justify the violent separation of a child from its human mother, which, when speaking of birds' nests, with admirable humanity commands charitable regard for the feelings even of an animal mother?"

There were no more than two hundred thousand Jews in all of America at the time of the Civil War. According to Simon Wolf in *The American Jew as Patriot Soldier, and Citizen*, over six thousand of them fought in the Union Army. There were in the Union Army at least nine Jewish Generals, eighteen Colonels, eight Lieutenant-Colonels, forty Majors, two hundred and five Captains, three hundred and twenty-five Lieutenants, forty-eight Adjutants and twenty-five Surgeons.

Seven Jews were awarded the Congressional Medal of Honor.

Jewish youth in the South enlisted in the Confederate Army. Some 1300 Jews are listed as having fought for the Confederate States.

Under a law passed by the United States Congress in 1861, only Christian clergymen were allowed to be military chaplains in the Union Army. Public pressure, organized by the Jews themselves, caused the law to be amended, and President Abraham Lincoln appointed several Jewish rabbis as Army Chaplains. When General Ulysses S. Grant, in the winter of 1862, issued his notorious Order No. 11, expelling Jews "as a class" from the Department of the Tennessee, a delegation of Jews, headed by Rabbi Isaac M. Wise, met with Lincoln and he immediately countermanded the order.

Reporting on the visit to President Lincoln, Rabbi Wise wrote in the *American Israelite*: "The President fully convinced us that he knows no distinction between Jews and Gentiles and that he feels no prejudice against any nationality and especially against the Israelites. We had little chance to say anything, the President being so splendidly eloquent on this occasion. He spoke like a simple, plain citizen and tried in various forms to convince us of the sincerity of his words on this matter."

RELATIONS OF THE AMERICAN GOVERNMENT WITH JEWS

True to its Democratic traditions the American Government has always fought for the rights of Jews all over the world, just as it has championed the rights of other minorities. In the famous Damascus affair, in 1840, where innocent Jews were falsely accused of using Christian blood for religious purposes, President Martin Van Buren instructed the American Consul in Egypt to defend the rights of the Jews. President Millard Fillmore and his secretary, Daniel Webster, protested to Switzerland against discrimination against Jews. President William H. Taft broke off commercial relations with Russia for discriminating against Jews. Finally, the United States, during the administration of President Truman, was the first government to recognize the newly established State of Israel.

FIVE WAVES OF JEWISH IMMIGRATION INTO THE UNITED STATES

The first arrival, as we have seen, was the landing of Jews in New Amsterdam. They came from Brazil and were mostly Spanish-Portuguese Jews. These were followed by other

Spanish-Portuguese Jews who settled in other parts of the United States.

Between 1848 and 1890, German and Western European Jews emigrated to the United States to escape oppression.

In 1890, large numbers of Eastern European Jews began to arrive from Lithuania, Poland and Russia. This lasted until the outbreak of the first World War in 1914, after which immigration was sharply curtailed.

WAVES OF JEWISH IMMIGRATION TO THE UNITED STATES

1880-1890	193,000
1890-1900	393,000
1901-1910	976,000

(more than 11 per cent of the total immigration)

Jewish population in the United States doubled in the decade, 1901-1910, rising from one million Jews in 1900 to over two million in 1910.

A major reason for the enormous size of the immigration from 1901-1910 was the pogrom wave of 1903-1906 in Russia. The pogrom wave began in Kishineff, Bessarabia, at Easter (April 19-21), 1903, when mobs instigated and abetted by tsarist authorities killed 47 Jews, wounded 437, and wrecked and looted 1500 stores and homes. Pogroms continued throughout Russia, reaching its height in Odessa, when from October 18 to 21, 1905, more than 300 Jews were killed, thousands wounded and 40,000 economically ruined.

In the five years 1904 to 1908, more than 482,000 Jews came to the United States from Russia.

In 1932, with the advent of Hitler and the consequent spread of Nazism in Europe, a fourth wave began, mostly of German Jews. After World War II in 1945, a fifth wave

87

began, of displaced persons and stateless Jews from Eastern Europe, who had been uprooted by the Nazis.

JEWISH POPULATION IN THE UNITED STATES

In 1800 there were 2,500 Jews in the United States; in 1840—15,000; in 1860—200,000; in 1880—250,000; in 1920—4,000,000; in 1953—5,000,000.

JEWISH CONTRIBUTION TO AMERICAN MILITARY FORCES

One hundred Jews, out of 2,000 Jews in America, fought in the War for Independence.

In the Civil War: In the Union Army—6,000 Jews; in the Confederate Army—1,200 Jews.

At least 4,000 Jews served with the U.S. Army in the Spanish-American War.

In World War I—200,000 Jews. Approximately 10,000 Jews had commissions in the Army, Navy and Marines.

In World War II—600,000 Jews served in the armed forces of the United States.

SOME OUTSTANDING AMERICAN JEWS OF THE 19TH AND 20TH CENTURIES

EMMA LAZARUS, poet. The Statue of Liberty carries her verses as its inscription, which reads in part:

> "Keep, ancient lands, your storied pomp," cries she
> With silent lips. "Give me your tired, your poor,
> Your huddled masses yearning to breathe free,
> The wretched refuse of your teeming shore.
> Send these, the homeless, tempest-tost to me.
> I lift my lamp beside the golden door."

REBECCA GRATZ, one of the pioneers of social work.

SIMON WOLF, writer, publicist and friend of presidents.

JACOB SCHIFF, philanthropist and fighter for Jewish rights.

DAVID LUBIN, organizer and American representative of the Institute of Agriculture.

OSCAR STRAUSS, Ambassador to Turkey, Secretary of Commerce in Theodore Roosevelt's cabinet.

NATHAN STRAUSS, his brother, philanthropist and humanitarian.

LOUIS MARSHALL, staunch fighter for Jewish rights both in America and throughout the world.

SAMUEL GOMPERS, father of American trade unionism and President of the American Federation of Labor.

LOUIS D. BRANDEIS, famous liberal Supreme Court Justice and leading American Zionist.

BENJAMIN CARDOZO, one of the greatest of American Supreme Court Justices.

HERBERT H. LEHMAN, United States Senator and three times Governor of the State of New York.

HENRY MORGENTHAU, SR., Ambassador to Turkey.

HENRY MORGENTHAU, JR., Secretary of the Treasury in Franklin D. Roosevelt's cabinet.

ALBERT EINSTEIN, world famous scientist who, born in Germany, abandoned that country during the Hitler regime and became a citizen of the United States.

CHARLES STEINMETZ, a close collaborator of Thomas A. Edison.

BRIGADIER GENERAL DAVID SARNOFF, a noted electrical engineer and President of the Radio Corporation of America.

PROF. J. OPPENHEIMER, PROF. ISADORE I. RABI and PROF. HAROLD C. UREY, noted scientists.

FELIX FRANKFURTER, member of U.S. Supreme Court.

AL JOLSON, PAUL MUNI, EDDIE CANTOR and many other actors, composers and singers, who enriched the American film and theatre.

It is also interesting to note that the clothing and moving-picture industries were developed almost exclusively by Jews.

THE SYNAGOGUE WHICH WAS PROCLAIMED A NATIONAL AMERICAN SHRINE

The Touro Synagogue in Newport, R. I., was established in 1763, by Rabbi Isaac Touro, a strong supporter of Washington. It was proclaimed a national American Shrine by the government under Franklin D. Roosevelt.

The son of Rabbi Isaac Touro, Judah Touro, is one of the best-known names in American Jewish history. He lived from 1775 to 1854, and in his will bequeathed $387,000 for various Jewish and non-Jewish institutions.

BEGINNINGS OF JEWISH EDUCATION

The first Jewish Sunday school was established by the Jews in 1838 in Philadelphia. It was organized by Rebecca Gratz, a well known social worker of that time.

The first daily Hebrew school was organized by the Shearit Israel Congregation in New York City in 1731.

The first Orthodox Rabbi in America was Rabbi Isaac Karrigal (late in the 18th Century). He was a friend of Ezra Stiles, president of Yale University.

The first Conservative Rabbi was Dr. Isaac Leeser (early part of the 19th Century).

Dr. Isaac M. Wise, Dr. Max Lilienthal and Dr. Stephen Wise were the leaders of Reform Judaism (19th and 20th Centuries).

Movement for an Independent Jewish Community (*1825*)

Mordecai Emanuel Noah, prominent in New York politics, a judge, surveyor of the Port of New York and American Consul in Tunis, sought to found an independent Jewish colony in America. He bought an island near Buffalo, which he called Ararat and invited Jews to settle there. But the response was very poor.

Most Jews have always stubbornly maintained that if a permanent Jewish community be established, it must be in the land of Israel.

Development of Hebrew and Jewish Education in America

When the first Hebrew school was opened in New York, in 1731, by the Shearit Israel congregation, it was a full-time day school. Later, it became an afternoon school, whose pupils attended public school in the morning.

In the 1940's, the all-day school idea was revived and gained much momentum. Not only in the big cities, but in many small communities, Yeshivot K'tanot, for elementary school age children and in some, even Mesiftot, for high school age children, were established.

It was believed for a long time that only cities with large Jewish populations could support Yeshivot K'tanot, but during the past fifteen years, in the smaller towns, the Yeshivot, or all-day schools, progressed so well that they became models for new Yeshivot. One such model is the Yeshiva in Elizabeth, New Jersey, which under the dynamic leadership of Rabbi P. Teitz, the originator of the now famous "Daf Ha'shavuah" or weekly Talmudic study over the radio, has become a model school for many schools to copy. During the past few years, three buildings worth close to $1,000,000 were built, to accommodate 300 children of elementary school and high school age. This Yeshiva has proven that any American Jewish community can support an educational project, if it proves useful to the children of their community.

East European Jews, on coming to America, opened Hadorim, (from the Hebrew "Heder"—room) small, one room afternoon schools, where the Torah was taught by old-fashioned methods. When Hebrew Maskilim, and other educated Hebrew teachers came to America, they organized modern Talmud Torahs (schools for the study of the Torah) in modern buildings, supervised by trained teachers. Later, some of these Talmud Torahs became all-day schools (Yeshivot K'tanot), where both religious and secular studies are taught.

As time and education progressed, higher schools of Jewish learning were opened. Among them are the Yeshiva University (Orthodox), the Jewish Theological Seminary (Conservative), the Hebrew Union College (Reform), the Rabbinical Seminary in Chicago, the Seminaries in Baltimore, Cleveland and Cincinnati, The Yiddish College, Dropsie College and others. There are also the Herzliah Academy, and other Hebrew high-schools. In addition, there are a number of Yiddish schools, where all subjects are taught in the Yiddish language. Some of these are supported by the Arbeiter Ring (Workmen's Circle), others by the Farband, a Jewish Social-Zionist organization.

At present, most Jewish schools in New York City (the city with the largest Jewish population in the United States—over 2,000,000)—Orthodox, Conservative, Reform and Yiddish—are under the supervision of the Bureau of Jewish Education of New York, under the direction of Dr. Alvin Schiff. In other cities, the schools are under the supervision of local Bureaus of Education, directed by the American Association for Jewish Education, headed by Dr. Shimon Frost. This organization strives to improve Hebrew Educaton all over the Unted States. There are, too, the Va'ad Hachinuch Ha'charedi Committee and the Torah U'Mesorah Committee, two orthodox organizations supervising a number of orthodox schools in a number of cities.

A Board of License supervises the issuing of licenses to teachers and to principals for all Hebrew Orthodox, Conservative, Reform and Yiddish schools affiliated with the Bureau of Jewish Education of New York. In other large communities, like Essex county of New Jersey, the Jewish Education Association of the county also has its own Board of License.

In addition, there are regional organizations of Hebrew educators and Hebrew principals, also the Jewish Educators Assembly.

Jewish Organizational Life in America

Jewish social and organized life in America took different turns with each new wave of immigration. When the Sephardic (Spanish) Jews arrived, they organized their social circles around their synagogue, cemetery, and educational activities.

The German Jews organized their social and religious life

93

on a more elaborate scale. They organized a seminary for Rabbis, fraternal organizations, and the HIAS (Hebrew Immigration Aid Society), which takes care of new immigrants. In addition they established a number of homes for the aged and orphans, etc., built a Y.M.H.A. for adolescents, and formed fraternal organizations like the Bnai Brith, etc.

The Eastern Jews seeking mutual assistance in a strange land, organized Landsmanshaften, organizations of immigrants from the same European town or district. The new immigrant joined his Landsmanshaft fraternal organization. There he found friends from his own home town. This gave him and his family a sense of security.

As the East European Jews became thoroughly Americanized, the German Jews, who had tended to remain aloof, began to mingle with them. Thus it came to pass that Polish and Russian Jews became leaders in organizations organized by German Jews, like the Bnai Brith, and Federation of Charities. West European and East European Jews now work together in educational, fraternal, social and charitable organizations. Each city in the United States with a sizcable Jewish population has its own committees to supervise its communal life.

Partial List of Jewish Religious, Social and Political Organizations

THE AMERICAN JEWISH CONGRESS, whose aim is to promote and preserve the democratic way of life, to encourage Jewish education and friendship, and to eliminate discrimination in every field.

THE AMERICAN JEWISH COMMITTEE, which combats anti-Semitism, and social and political inequality.

BNAI BRITH, a fraternal order, founded in 1843 with the

purpose of furthering social, cultural and philanthropic work for Jews of all shades of religious opinion. The Anti-Defamation League, as part of its work, combats anti-Semitism in the United States. The Hillel foundation of the Bnai Brith helps Jewish students spiritually on many college campuses throughout the country.

BNAI AKIBA, a religious youth organization.

BRITH TRUMPELDOR, a Zionist organization with a Revisionist program.

THE FARBAND, a fraternal labor Zionist organization.

FEDERATION OF JEWISH CHARITIES, an organization composed of 116 health and social agencies for the purpose of serving the medical, social, educational and religious needs of men, women and children.

THE HABONIM, a Zionist youth organization which maintains training camps for boys and girls interested in pioneer life in Israel. It also conducts extensive cultural Zionist activity.

HADASSAH, a women's organization which provides medical, social, cultural, and welfare assistance to the people of Israel. It also provides an extensive educational program for its members in the United States.

HAPOEL HAMIZRACHI, a religious, social Zionist, labor organization.

HISTADRUT IVRIT, a national organization for Hebrew culture and for the promotion of Hebrew language study and literature. It publishes *Hadoar*, a Hebrew weekly, and Hebrew books and pamphlets.

THE INTERCOLLEGIATE ZIONIST FEDERATION, composed of Jewish college students, whose aim is Zionist education and activity.

JEWISH AGRICULTURAL SOCIETY, an organization which

encourages farming among Jews by offering practical help and realistic advice.

JEWISH BOARD OF GUARDIANS, specializes in child guidance and offers help to both children and parents in solving their social problems.

JEWISH FAMILY SERVICE, a social service organization for the improvement of Jewish family life.

JEWISH SABBATH ALLIANCE, an organization which furthers the observance of Sabbath among employers and employees in America.

JEWISH WAR VETERANS.

THE JOINT DISTRIBUTION COMMITTEE, an organization which provides help for immigrants and displaced persons all over the world.

MIZRACHI, an organization which promotes the building of Israel along religious lines.

NATIONAL FEDERATION OF TEMPLE BROTHERHOODS AND SISTERHOODS, an affiliate of the Union of American Hebrew Congregations.

NATIONAL COUNCIL OF JEWISH WOMEN, with hundreds of branches all over the country. Its purpose is to provide social, religious, educational and medical services to needy Jews all over the world.

IVRIAH, an organization of women to promote Hebrew education among Jewish mothers and children.

NATIONAL JEWISH WELFARE BOARD, an organization of hundreds of affiliated Jewish community centers, for the purpose of coordinating Jewish social life all over the United States and abroad, in civil organizations, the armed services, in religion and education.

NATIONAL COUNCIL OF YOUNG ISRAEL, seeks to strengthen

synagogue activities, and youth programs under synagogue auspices.

WOMEN'S MIZRACHI, an organization whose purpose is to help develop the land of Israel along the precepts of the Torah.

THE WORKMEN'S CIRCLE, a socialist fraternal organization, active in the cultural and social development of its members.

UNION OF AMERICAN HEBREW CONGREGATIONS, a union of Reform Temples and Centers all over the country.

UNION OF ORTHODOX JEWISH CONGREGATIONS, a national body of Orthodox synagogues in the United States, is concerned with the betterment of synagogue and community life, along Orthodox lines.

UNITED SYNAGOGUE, a union of all Conservative Temples and Centers in the United States. With its affiliate— *The National Women's League*—it is concerned with the betterment of community life along Conservative lines.

YOUNG JUDEA, an organization which develops an understanding and a love for Jewish customs and Zionist ideas, among Jewish youth.

YOUNG MEN'S AND YOUNG WOMEN'S HEBREW ASSOCIATIONS, organizations whose purpose is to provide social and cultural activities and opportunities for young Jewish men and women.

THE ZIONIST ORGANIZATION OF AMERICA, whose aim it is to help build the land of Israel.

CHAPTER FIVE

THE LAND OF ISRAEL

HISTORY

In ancient times, the Israel we know today was the land of the Hitim or Hittites, a people related to the Scythians, the ancient Slavs. It was later called the land of Canaan, from the Canaanites, who had driven out the Hittites. The Israel‑ites conquered it from the Canaanites. Assyria conquered the northern part, the area of the ten tribes of Israel; Babylonia conquered the area of the two-and-a-half tribes, Judea. Persia conquered the land from Babylon. Alexander the Great con‑quered it from the Persians.

Judea later became part of Egypt under the Ptolemies. The Seleucid Greeks took it from the Ptolemies. The Jews regained independence from the Seleucids in the second Cen‑tury B.C.E. The land was conquered by Rome in 70 C.E. The Arabs took the land from Rome. Crusaders ruled it for a brief period and then it was retaken by the Arabs. The Turks then took it from he Arabs and held it until 1917. England conquered it from the Turks and held it until 1948. In 1948 it became the independent State of Israel.

After the unsuccessful revolt of Bar Kochba in 132 C.E., the Romans called it Palestine, to indicate to the Jews that they had lost all claim to the land of Israel. The name Pales‑tine came from the ancient Philistines, who once occupied part of the land on the Mediterranean. But the name "Israel" could not be eradicated. The Israelites had developed a spiritual culture, not only strong enough to perpetuate their identity but to enrich the entire world. It was in the land of Israel that the idea of one God was introduced and passed on to the rest of humanity.

Rabbi Johanan Ben Zakkai, and other Sages played an important role in preserving spiritual unity. The former asked and received permission from the Roman Emperor, Vespasian, in whose reign the Roman conquest occurred, to build a Talmudic academy in Yavne. This academy became the spiritual center for the dispersed Jews and kept strong their ties with Israel.

The Sages also directed that Jews should mention Zion, Jerusalem and the Temple in their prayers three times a day. In this way they kept alive the Jewish love for Zion. In the 19th Century, the Maskilim began to write poems, novels and articles advocating the idea of Zionism.

ISRAEL ESTABLISHED

During World War I, two former Russian officers, Vladimir Jabotinsky (a well-known writer and lecturer in a number of languages), and Joseph Trumpeldor (who died in Israel fighting the attacking Arabs), organized the Jewish Legion, to fight with the British in Palestine. The British sent them to battle in Turkey instead.

To show appreciation for the Legion, England through her foreign secretary, Lord Balfour, issued a proclamation in 1917 which promised help in establishing a home for the Jews in Palestine. The Declaration was issued also as a result of the great contribution of Dr. Chaim Weizmann, a renowned scientist, to the war effort. Weizmann was to become Israel's first president.

When the war ended, England appointed Sir Herbert Samuel as her first high.commissioner in Palestine. The Jews soon discovered that England was not sincere in her intentions. Samuel favored the Arabs. Trans-Jordan was severed from Palestine. The Arab Huseini, an arch-enemy of the Jews, was made Grand-Mufti (high spiritual official of the Arabs). Restrictions were placed on the immigration of Jews into Palestine. In many sections Jews were forbidden to purchase land.

A Jewish underground movement sprang up. It was highly organized, well-led and well-armed. This underground movement harassed the British until, on May 14th, 1948, England gave up Palestine. On the same day the Independent State of Israel was proclaimed by David Ben Gurion, leader of the Mapai party. He became the first Prime Minister of the new state, with Moshe Sharett as its first foreign minister, and Dr. Chaim Weizmann as its first President. After the Israeli proclamation of independence, seven Arab nations, outnumbering the Jews seventy to one, attacked the infant state. The Jews fought heroically and victoriously. In 1949 Israel was admitted to the United Nations.

GEOGRAPHY OF ISRAEL

The area of the land of Israel is 8048 square miles or approximately the size of the state of New Jersey. The land is measured by dunans (one dunan equals one-quarter acre).

BOUNDARIES On the North: Lebanon and Syria; East, Trans-Jordan; South, Egypt; West, the Mediterranean Sea.

PRINCIPAL RIVERS   Jordan (from Hebrew—Yarod—to go down): 73 miles (within Israeli territory); Yarkon (from Hebrew—Yarok—green): 16.1 miles; Kishon: 8.1 miles.

LAKES   Dead Sea or Salt Sea: 102 square miles (within Israeli territory); Sea of Galilee or Lake Kineret: 63.7 square miles; Lake of Huleh or water of Merom: 5.4 square miles—a source of malaria, it was drained and turned into fertile farmland.

REGIONS

1. *Galilee*: hilly country. Main cities, Safed (population 15,000); Holy Christian city, Nazareth (57,000); Acre (36,000).
2. *Haifa Bay area*: main city, Haifa, from Hebrew "Hof," bank of sea (227,900).
3. *The Emek*: main city, Afula (18,800).
4. *Jordan Valley*: main city, Tiberias, resort center (27,500).
5. *The Sharon plain*: main cities, Hedera (36,200); Nathania, center of diamond and movie industries (86,000); Jaffa-Tel Aviv, meaning hill of spring (394,000); Ramleh (37,500); Lod (or Lydda), with its airport (37,000); and Rehobot, with its famous Weizmann Institute (54,500).
6. *Hill area of Judea*: main city and capital of Israel, Jerusalem (336,000).
7. *The Negev or Southern part of Israel*: main city, Beer-Sheba (99,000).

HIGHEST ALTITUDE   3,962 feet, Mt. Atzmon, Galilee.

LOWEST LAND LEVEL   minus 1,286 feet, shores of Dead Sea (lowest point in world).

TEMPERATURE   Coldest (in January) 44.6 F.; Hottest (in August) 93.9 F.

CLIMATE   Temperate to sub-tropical.

RAINFALL   Driest area (Elath, Negev) .8 inches; Wettest area (Upper Galilee) 42.5 inches.

PORTS   Haifa (best in middle East), Tel-Aviv, Elath (on Red Sea).

NATURAL RESOURCES   Potash, caustic soda, magnesium, bromine, rock phosphates, ceramic clays, glass sand, feldspar, manganese, copper, iron, mica. Various companies have been drilling for oil in different sections of the land; promising results have already been obtained.

ECONOMY, INDUSTRY, AGRICULTURE

In ancient days Israel was considered a land flowing with milk and honey. After the Jews were exiled from their land, it lay waste for centuries. The Arabs let the desert advance over the land. With the return of the modern Jew, the land is again beginning to flourish. It is being developed into a highly industrialized country. It produces fertilizers and electricity. It has a metal industry, a building industry, textiles, food processing, diamond industry, chemicals, petroleum by-products, paints, oils, detergents, paper products, plastics, pharmaceuticals, automobile parts, tires, rubber products, leather, furniture, sanitary equipment, refrigerators, machinery, watches, precision instruments, and many others. A billion-dollar munitions industry is a recent addition.

EXPORTS   Among Israel's main exports are citrus fruits and their by-products.

AGRICULTURAL PRODUCTION in grain, green fodder, hay,

peanuts, sunflowers, tobacco, grapes, fruits, olives, eggs, milk, poultry, cotton, flax, etc. is increasing every year. A newly developed fishing industry is making great strides.

IRRIGATION AND DAIRY PRODUCTION   The Negev in ancient days was the breadbasket of the Middle East. After the expulsion of the Jews, however, it became a desert. It was believed that not even grass could grow there. With modern irrigation methods (like the 60 mile pipeline from the Yarkon river in the North), it is again becoming a fertile land. In the Moshavot (villages based on private land ownership), in Kibbutzim (collective settlements), Moshvei Ovdim (workers' cooperative settlements), Moshavim (smallholders' settlements), Moshavim Shitufim (settlements based on collective ownership or work) the dairy and vegetable industries are being developed. On these, and on Arab farms as well, vegetable gardens, chicken farms, and dairy products are making the land self-sustaining.

TRANSPORTATION   The railways, shipping ports (with their greatly expanded merchant marine), air fields of Lydda and Haifa, Dov airport and Elat, the airlines of El-Al, Arkia and Chim, also the bus lines and commercial vehicles, greatly help in developing the Israeli economy.

THE ISRAELI POSTAL SYSTEM is a member of the International Postal Union, with eighty-six post offices throughout the country. The Telephone System, with its sixty-five exchanges, has direct telegraph communications with fifty countries. (See Addenda, p. 223.)

FINANCES are based on the shekel, which is the official currency of the country (equal to about 60 cents at the present rate of exchange). (See Addenda p. 223.)

Israel has 28 commercial and 97 co-operative banks in its financial system. It also has seven industrial and trade organizations, and six organizations of labor and six of agriculture.

ARMY   All these gains are protected by the Israeli army, the Haganah (from the Hebrew, L'hagin, to defend), a military force which combines the best ancient tactical ideas with modern methods and equipment.

CULTURAL LIFE

When the first Jewish pioneers settled in Palestine at the beginning of the twentieth Century, Hebrew as a spoken language had been forgotten by the Jews, who spoke the languages of the countries in which they lived, or languages which they had developed, such as Yiddish, or Ladino. Ladino is based on Spanish and is still spoken by descendants of Jewish exiles from Spain and Portugal, who had found refuge in countries under Turkish rule.

Hebrew was used only for prayer and specialized study. In the beginning of the twentieth Century, the Hebrew scholar, Eliezer Ben Yehudah, set out to revive Hebrew as a spoken tongue and adapt it to modern-day needs. He wrote a modern Hebrew dictionary and simplified the vocabulary. His idea spread rapidly and, after only a quarter of a century, Hebrew ceased to be a dead language. This revival is considered a modern miracle. Hebrew is now the official language of Israel, and is spoken fluently by Jews in many parts of the world.

In terms of continuity, culture in Israel never ceased, as witness the Yeshivot and religious schools of the land. Moses began universal, cultural training of the Jews which continued through the ages. In the days of the Temple, priests and Levites continued this cultural training when Jews visited the Temple three times a year, as prescribed by law. The Kohanim and Levites traveled through the land to give instruction.

After the destruction of the 2nd Temple, the sages organized schools wherever there was a Jewish population. During the Middle Ages the Jews were the only people with a highly literate population. Close to 98 per cent could read and write. The most honored people among Jews were the scholars.

The modern culture of Israel began, a generation ago, with the revival of Hebrew as a spoken language. Today, in 1955, under the supervision of the Ministry of Education there are 900 elementary schools, 80 high schools, 40 agricultural schools, 50 vocational training schools, 250 evening schools, 18 teachers' colleges, a large number of army schools and Ulpanim schools for adults, 110 Arab schools. The Hebrew University in Jerusalem includes a Medical School, a Dental School, and a School of Pharmacy. There are also: The Israel Institute of Technology (with departments in Civil Engineering, Architecture, Mechanical Engineering, Electrical Engineering, Chemical Engineering and Sciences; the Schools of Law and Economics in Haifa and in Tel Aviv; the Weizmann Institute of Science in Rehobot (a post-graduate course of study in pure science and research); the Bar Ilan University and many religious schools and Yeshivot. A large number of newspapers and magazines (23 daily, 96 weekly, 116 monthly are read in Israel, and thousands of Hebrew and other language books are published there. The Israelis are among the most avid readers of literature in the world. Whenever they establish a new settlement, the first organizations are a nursery and a library.

There are eight theaters in Israel, not counting the numerous motion picture houses where the best international pictures are shown. The country has 18 music conservatories 65 school orchestras, a large number of musical institution. including the Israeli Philharmonic Orchestra (organized by Bronislaw Huberman, famous violinist). There are eight large libraries in the country and many libraries in almost every town and village.

There are six museums, besides the art galleries in Tel Aviv, Jerusalem, and Haifa.

The Kol Israel Radio station broadcasts in Hebrew, Yiddish, French, English, Ladino, Rumanian, Russian, Hungarian, Turkish, Persian, etc. The dances and songs composed by Israeli composers and by Sabras (native-born), are sung and danced by Jewish youth all over the world.

Social Welfare

The foundation of Israel's medical service was laid years ago by two organizations: The Hadassah Medical Organization (organized by Henrietta Szold of America), and the Kupat Cholim (workers' fund).

By the end of 1953, there were 87 hospitals in Israel, including a government hospital under the Ministry of Health. Hadassah and Kupat Cholim had about 900 clinics and dispensaries, 369 mother and child care centers, and about ten mental hospitals. The Malben Institution for handicapped immigrants had 8 hospitals, a T.B. center, 15 old-age homes, a village for blind people, a home for retarded children and

23 workshops for handicapped people, besides the large number of private institutions, mobile hospitals and Red Magen-David ambulances, which serve Jews and Arabs alike. (See Addenda, p. 223.)

POLITICAL LIFE

The Government of Israel is based on the parliamentary system of democratic proportional representation. The Executive or Cabinet is responsible to the Knesset (Parliament). There are 120 deputies in the Knesset representing close to fifteen parties. Elections are by secret ballot and are based on universal suffrage.

The President is elected by the Knesset and has only limited power. The flag of Israel consists of a white background (symbol of peace), with two blue stripes (symbol of hope), and the star or shield of David. The national hymn is "Hatikvah" (Hope), with verse written by Imber and music adapted from Smetana's "The Moldau."

THE POLITICAL PARTIES of Israel are:

Mapai, Israel right-wing labor party.

Mapam, left-wing labor party.

General Zionists, mostly of middle-class element.

Progressive Zionists, a wing of the General Zionists.

Mizrachi party, religious party.

Hapoel Hamizrachi, religious labor party.

Revisionists or the *Herut.*

The *Agudat Israel* with the *Poale-Agudat Israel,* ultra-orthodox.

Israel Arab Democrats, for improvement of conditions of the Arab population.

The Communist party.

Israel Association of Yemenites, an organization of Yemenite Jews.

Progress and Work party and also *Farmers and Development party,* both Arab parties. (See also p. 31.)

THE CONSTITUTIONAL RIGHTS in Israel provide:

1. No death penalty.
2. Freedom from arrest without a warrant.
3. Freedom of religion, freedom from discrimination on account of race, religion, language or sex.
4. Freedom of speech, press and assembly.
5. Freedom of employment and social security.
6. Right of workers to form and join trade unions.
7. Right to health and educational facilities.

JUDICIARY SYSTEM consists of City courts, District courts and the Highest (Supreme) Court. The Rabbinical Courts have jurisdiction over religious matters, including marriage and divorce. The Muslim court has jurisdiction over Muslim religious matters.

Since ancient days, the tiny land of Israel has been a bone of contention between powerful neighbor empires. First it was Syria and Egypt, then Assyria and Egypt, then Babylon and Egypt, Persia and Egypt, Greece and Egypt, Rome and Parthia, Arabs and the Crusaders, Turkey and England, England and the Jews. This kind of conflict has continued to the present day.

Economic strength also means political strength, and this is what Israel is trying to achieve. At present, the country is forced to maintain a large army, but as soon as peace is established with the Arabs, expenditures now diverted to the army will go to industrial, agricultural, educational, cultural and social purposes. As a member of the United Nations, Israel is respected politically and spiritually. The new State of Israel projects an excellent example of a dynamic, creative, democratic country to the rest of the world. Today, as in past centuries, Israel is again considered the gateway to the East.

CHAPTER SIX

WOMEN IN ANCIENT JEWISH LIFE

The status of woman in Jewish life was very high. She was never treated as a slave.

Sarah, the wife of Abraham, took an equal part with him in spreading the belief in one God. It was because of the wisdom and influence of their wives that Rabbi Akiba and Rabbi Meir took their places among the great Sages of Israel. The daughters of Zelophechad were awarded their father's land, thus establishing the right of Jewish women to inherit and own property.

Many Sages have described women as having stronger characters than men, as in the case of Beruria, wife of Rabbi Meir. It is told that on a Sabbath day, the two sons of Rabbi Meir died suddenly. As it is against the law to mourn on the Sabbath, Beruria hid the bodies of her sons and waited until nightfall to inform her husband of the misfortune.

The Sages advise that every Jew honor his mother equally with his father, in keeping with the Fifth Commandment; and to honor his wife as well. They describe a man without a wife as being like unto a dead man. A man's home, they say, consists of his wife. If a husband is tall and his wife is short, he should bend down and whisper in her ear (Itshach Gutzah, Gahin V'tilchash). This is interpreted to mean that a husband should hold no secrets from his wife.

The Jewish woman was assigned fewer religious laws to observe, not because of discrimination, but because of the pressure of household duties. The privilege of reciting the blessing over candles is assigned to her, for she is considered the foundation of the home.

The Jewish woman has been considered the business equal of her husband. In time of persecution she frequently replaced her husband as the breadwinner of the family.

Among the women who played important roles in early Jewish history were:

ADA OR EDITH

Ada or Edith was the name of Lot's wife who was turned into a pillar of salt. When God destroyed the evil cities of Sodom and Gomorrah, He saved Lot, the nephew of Abraham. The angel sent by God to save Lot and his family warned them not to look back. Lot's wife, however, disregarded this warning. For this and other evil deeds, she was turned into a pillar of salt.

The salt here symbolizes Edith's treachery. True to the traditions of Sodom and Gomorrah, she had decided to betray her husband Lot and his guests. She had planned to do this under the pretext of borrowing salt from a neighbor.

ZULEIKA

Zuleika was the wife of Potiphar who purchased Joseph as his slave. Through false accusations she brought about Joseph's imprisonment.

BATHIA

When Pharaoh of Egypt ordered all the new-born Jewish boys thrown into the Nile River, the infant Moses was placed by his mother in a basket, and left on the river-bank. When Princess Bathia, a daughter of the king, came there to bathe, she found the basket, and had the infant raised as a member of the royal family.

MIRIAM
Miriam, the sister of Moses, was a great women's leader and a prophetess.

ZIPPORAH
Moses sought refuge in the land of Midian after he killed a brutal Egyptian overseer. There he married Zipporah, youngest daughter of the priest of Midian, Jethro. She had two sons, Gershom and Eliezer.

NAOMI AND RUTH
In the days of the Judges, a Jewish family moved to Moab from Israel because of famine. The two sons of the family married Moabite women, both of whom were princesses. The sons died and the mother-in-law Naomi, decided to return to Israel. Ruth, one of her daughters-in-law, insisted on going with her. In Israel, they lived in poverty, gleaning the fields for corn that had dropped from the reapers' sheaves. One day Boaz, the richest man in the country, saw Ruth gathering corn, fell in love with her and married her. King David was their great-grandson. To this day Ruth is honored as the ancestress of the greatest Jewish hero. In honor of her fidelity to her chosen religion, the scroll of Ruth is read on Shavuot, which is the day of the giving of the Torah.

DEBORAH AND HULDA
Deborah was famous as a judge, military leader and prophetess. Hulda (during the first Temple) was also a prophetess.

Since only a prophet was considered perfect, it is important to note here that in Jewish annals women as well as men achieved perfection and equality.

TZLILPONITH

Tzlilponith was the mother of the hero, Samson.

HANNAH

Hannah once came to the Tabernacle to pray for the birth of a son. Because her problem was so deeply personal, she prayed modestly in silence, instead of in a loud voice, as was then the custom. The High Priest Eli, seeing her standing in a corner whispering, thought she was mad or drunk, until she explained her reason to the priest. Her prayers were answered, for she had a son, Samuel, who became one of the greatest prophets and leaders of the Jews. In honor of Samuel and his mother, silent prayer was introduced into the service. To this day, the most important prayers are chanted in the synagogue in a low, whispered voice. It is said that prayer, spoken in a low voice, is best heard by God.

ESTHER (350 B.C.E.)

Esther, wife of Ahasuerus, king of Persia, became queen after he divorced his first wife Vashti. She saved the Jews from the hands of Haman the prime minister, who planned the extermination of the Jews. (*See* section on Holidays, Purim.)

JUDITH

Judith of Bethulia killed Holofernes, the Babylonian commander who besieged Judea, and whose death led to the defeat of the Babylonian army.

QUEEN OF SHEBA

The Queen of Sheba, whose name was Balkis, was a friend of King Solomon.

QUEEN SHLOMITH ALEXANDRA (*76 B.C.E.*)

The wife of Alexander Janai, the Hasmonean king of Judea, she organized Jewish schools throughout the land, with the help of her brother, the Sage Simon Ben Shetah.

CHAPTER SEVEN

FAMOUS FIRSTS IN JEWISH HISTORY

This chapter provides information that is both interesting and amusing. It can easily be incorporated into a quiz game for young and old.

THE FIRST MOTHER: Eve.

THE FIRST SHEPHERD: Abel, the son of Adam and Eve.

THE FIRST FARMER: Cain, the brother of Abel.

THE FIRST MURDERER: Cain, who killed his brother Abel.

THE FIRST BOAT BUILDER: Noah, who built the Ark.

THE FIRST TO DISCOVER FIRE: Adam.

THE FIRST DRUNKARD: Noah, who planted grapes after the Flood, made wine, and often got drunk.

THE FIRST SHLUMIEL: Lemech (Today, Shlumiel and Lemech are synonymous terms).

THE FIRST MUSICIAN: Jubal, son of Lemech.

THE FIRST BLACKSMITH: Tubal Cain, also son of Lemech.

THE FIRST MATCHMAKER: Eliezer, the chief servant of Abraham, whose matchmaking efforts are the first recorded in history. He was sent by Abraham to Mesopotamia to find a wife for Isaac. Through his clever matchmaking Eliezer brought Rebecca to Isaac.

THE FIRST TO DISCOVER THE CONCEPT OF ONE GOD: Abraham, whose father Terach, was a maker of idols. When

Abraham came to the realization that there was only one God, he smashed his father's idols.

THE FIRST HEBREW: Abraham, who crossed the Euphrates River from Mesopotamia into the land of Canaan. "Avor" in Hebrew means to cross. Ivri means, the one who crossed. The Mesopotamians and Canaanites called Abraham and his followers Habiri.

THE FIRST ISRAELITE: Jacob, who as the Bible tells us, wrestled with an angel. The angel blessed him and called him Israel (Yisroel), meaning one who has successfully wrestled with a prince of God.

THE FIRST JEW: Judah, or Yehudah, son of Jacob. Judah means to thank God. Jew is an abbreviation of Judah.

THE FIRST SANDWICH MAKER: Hillel (70 B.C.E.), called the "old one." He originated the custom of making a sandwich of Matzoh and bitter herbs to be eaten during the Seder nights on Passover, as commanded in the Bible. To this day it is a part of traditional Passover observance.

THE FIRST FAMOUS RECORDED STUTTERER: According to the Sages, Moses having burned his tongue in childhood, remained a stutterer for the rest of his life. The story goes that when Moses, as a child, placed the king's crown on his head, Pharaoh wished to discover whether Moses was so smart that he might take his kingdom away from him, as predicted by a magician. Gold and burning coal were placed in front of the infant Moses. Moses wished to take the gold, but, according to legend, an angel pushed his hand toward the burning coal. . . . Little Moses put his burned fingers into his mouth and burned his tongue.

THE FIRST KING OF ISRAEL: Saul.

THE FIRST KING OF JUDAH: David.

THE FIRST KING OF THE TEN TRIBES: Jeroboam.

THE FIRST EAVESDROPPER: Sarah, the wife of Abraham, who eavesdropped when the angels visited Abraham in his tent.

THE FIRST WOMEN TO DEMAND PROPERTY RIGHTS: The daughters of Zelophechad.

THE FIRST JEW TO WIN EQUAL RIGHTS IN AMERICA: Asher Levy of New Amsterdam.

THE FIRST WOMAN WHOSE CONSENT FOR MARRIAGE WAS ASKED: Rebecca. Before Rebecca agreed to marry Isaac, she established the previously unheard-of precedent of requiring her personal consent.

THE FIRST JEW TO DIE IN THE AMERICAN WAR FOR INDEPENDENCE: Francis Salvador of South Carolina.

Part Two

JEWISH RELIGION
ETHICS
AND
CULTURE

CHAPTER EIGHT

JEWISH RELIGION AND CULTURE

In this second section of the book an account and simple explanation of the great Jewish cultural heritage of almost three thousand years, is given.

We begin with the earliest part, the Pentateuch, follow with the Prophets and their spiritual sermons, and the later writings of the Second Temple period. Then, the development of the gigantic Code of laws, the Talmud, which took a thousand years to write and compile. It is cosmopolitan in character, since it was written by sages of different countries, and the post-Talmudic commentaries include sages of practically every country of Europe, Asia and Africa. It contains, not only law, but folklore, science, etc. Then follows the literature of the Middle Ages. At a time when dark clouds of superstition, ignorance and violence descended on Europe, the Jews, though caught in the grinding of that maelstrom, through their great belief in God and their hope, managed to create a colossal cultural literature of thousands of volumes.

The Jewish literature of the 18th, 19th, and 20th Centuries is also gigantic in its form. It is amazing that a little nation, spread over all countries of the world, oppressed and driven, could create such a gigantic cultural inheritance. It is truly miraculous.

TANACH

The Torah, the Prophets and the Ketuvim (Hagiographa) together form the monumental work called the Tanach. Tanach is an abbreviation of: "T" for Torah, "N" for Neviim (Prophets), "CH" or "K" for Ketuvim.

THE TORAH (*Written Law*)

The Torah refers to the Pentateuch or Five Books of Moses. The word "Torah" comes from the Hebrew, "L'horoth," meaning to teach. The Torah teaches us how to regulate our daily existence in the relationships of man to God, and of man to man. It is written on scrolls of parchment and consists of the following books:

> GENESIS (BERESHITH): From Creation through the lives of the three Patriarchs, Abraham, Isaac and Jacob.
>
> EXODUS (SHMOTH): Slavery, Exodus from Egypt and principal laws.
>
> LEVITICUS (VAYIKRA): Laws concerning the Tabernacle and sacrifices.
>
> NUMBERS (BAMIDBAR): Wanderings in the desert.
>
> DEUTERONOMY (DEVARIM): Repetition of the laws.

The Torah is divided into 54 sections or portions called Sedroth, containing 5,845 sentences, 79,976 words, 304,805 letters.

JEWISH LIFE IN THE DESERT (*As organized by Moses according to the Torah*)

When Moses led the Jewish slaves out of Egypt, they were completely disorganized. According to the law of God, given to him on Mt. Sinai, Moses created the following organizations:

JUDICIARY

The head of the family (which consisted of many people) was its judge. As in all societies of free men, they were provided a higher or supreme court, formed by Moses and the council of elders. When the Jews entered the Promised Land, however, certain changes took place. Military leaders, then kings, became judges. Later on the Great Council or Assembly, established by Ezra, took over. Then, during the period of the Second Temple, the Great Sanhedrin was established as the chief judiciary body. This group, in turn, after the destruction of the Second Temple, gave way to the heads of Talmudic Academies as the chief religious judges.

MILITARY

The army was organized in groups of tens, hundreds, thousands and tens of thousands, each group commanded by an officer. The tribal chief commanded a tribal group analagous to a modern army corps. The commander-in-chief was Moses, with Joshua as his chief of staff. When Moses died, Joshua succeeded him.

Moses realized that, in the desert, he must have a strong organization. To effect this he combined the judiciary powers with the military, but made sure that later, in the land of Israel, these powers would be separated. Thus, in Israel, the priests and the prophets became the religious judges while the kings became the civil and military judges.

EDUCATION

The Priests and Levites were appointed as teachers to the nation and were supported and provided for by the people.

With characteristic forethought, the Torah stipulated that these teachers (Kohanim and Levites) could own no property. Moses, in carrying out this edict, prevented the formation of an intellectual aristocracy living apart from the people.

ECONOMY

Life in the desert was austere. According to the Torah, Moses established a simple form of taxation. There was the *Teruma Gedola* or tax from the gross income. It amounted to two per cent of the gross income, and went to the Kohanim. Then there was the *Ma'aser* or ten per cent of the remainder, which belonged to the Levites. From this *Ma'aser,* the Levites were required to give ten per cent to the Kohanim. It was called *Terumath Ma'aser.* Thus every Israelite was taxed approximately twelve per cent of his gross income. These taxes were continued when the Jews settled in Israel. For the building of the Tabernacle, or other emergencies, special assessments were made. Otherwise, twelve per cent was the most paid. There were also voluntary taxes for the benefit of the poor. This was known as *Leket* (gathering), *Shikcha* (forgetting) and *Peah* (corner). The landowner was required to leave a corner of his field unharvested, so that the poor might gather food there and not have to beg or suffer the humiliation of asking for charity.

One of the most curious taxes was the *Ma'aser Sheni* (second year *Ma'aser* tax). This was a stipulation that every Israelite reserve ten per cent of his income after regular taxes, for his own cultural benefit and entertainment. This money, however, had to be spent in Jerusalem during visits to the Holy Temple. Once every three years, instead of the visit to

Jerusalem, it was customary to contribute this personal tax to the poor. This tax was called *Ma'aser Ani.*

According to the directives of the Torah, portions of some of the sacrifices brought into the Tabernacle and later into the Temple, belonged to the Priests and their families. The Torah commanded the Jews to bring a number of sacrifices into the Tabernacle, some of which were:

Tamid: daily offering   *Chatoth*: sin offering
Olah: burnt offering   *Asham*: guilt offering
Mincha: afternoon offering   *Todah*: thanks offering
Shelamim: peace offering   Special Holiday offerings

According to the law of the Torah, Moses established the following systems:

THE MONETARY SYSTEM

- 1 Kikar (talent): equal to 120 Mona
- 1 Mona: 25 Selaim
- 1 Selah: 2 Shekalim
- 1 Shekel (equivalent to a dollar): 2 Bekaim
- 1 Bekah: 2 Zuzim
- 1 Zuz: 5 Gerah
- 1 Gerah: 5 Perutoth

THE DRY MEASURE SYSTEM

- 1 Kohr: equal to 6 Eifa and 2 Sa'ah
- 1 Eifa: 10 Omer
- 1 Omer: 43 and 1/5 eggs
- 1 Eifa: 3 Sa'ah
- 1 Sa'ah: 6 Kabin

1 Kav: 4 Lugin

An olive was the smallest measure.

LIQUIDS

1 Hin: equal to 4 quarters hin.

A quarter hin: 3 Lugin

DISTANCE

1 Parsah: equal to approximately one mile

1 Ammah (cubit): 2/3 of a yard or 6 Tefachim

1 Tefach: 2 Komotzim

1 Kometz: 2 Fingerwidths

CIVIL CODE

The civil code enacted by Moses is, in certain respects, remarkably advanced.

Into a world where most civilized nations considered slaves as animals, Moses introduced a code of human rights for everybody, including slaves, which was truly revolutionary for its time. It included a heretofore unknown stipulation for limitation of work. A slave had to rest on the Sabbath and he was freed after six years (Exodus).

In those days, a master had to think twice about accepting a man as a slave, since it was incumbent upon the master to support the slave's family so long as the man worked for him. The Bible is filled with reminders to the Jews that they were once slaves in Egypt and that they must value their freedom and the freedom of strangers in their midst. In many ways Moses' civil code was the great-grandfather of modern social legislation.

Moses advocated full democracy. According to the command of the Torah, the concept that the most able man

128

should be the leader, that the right to rule should n♀t be hereditary, came into being at that time. (This concept has become widely accepted only in modern times.) Moses passed over his own mediocre sons (Gershom and Eliezer) and groomed Joshua, the son of Nun, as the leader to succeed him.

Joshua went a step further and did not appoint a successor. After his death the tribes selected their own leaders. For two hundred years they had their own judges, uniting only in times of common peril. The prophet Samuel, following the precepts of the Torah, at first refused to give the people a king, maintaining that God is the King of all people.

The death penalty was imposed for premeditated murder, striking and hurting one's parents, kidnapping a person and selling him into slavery, demagoguery which misled the people, adultery, and other crimes.

Special protection was given to those committing accidental murder. Six border cities supervised by Levites were established for that purpose. Here they were sheltered and protected against vengeance by the family of the unfortunate victim. Thus vendetta, or further bloodshed was prevented.

The worker had to receive his pay as soon as his work was completed. Compensation to workers for injury was also provided for in the Torah and enacted in Moses' Civil Code.

It is important to note that the Bible's statement "an eye for an eye" was not meant literally. The defendant had to pay compensation for permanent injury, for the cost of a doctor, the loss of time from work and for the suffering experienced by the plaintiff. (This principle is used in modern law.) It was further decreed that if a master injured a slave, the latter was to be given his freedom.

According to the institution of Yovel (fifty-year period) a

man could not sell his land forever. When the Yovel or fifty-year period was proclaimed, all sold land reverted to its original owner or to his heirs. Also the slaves went free.

According to the institution of Shemita (six-year period), land could be worked for six years, but had to be rested for the entire seventh year for the purposes of resuscitation. Slaves also had to be set free and all debts cancelled.

Since most people found it difficult to negotiate a loan near the end of the Shemita termination date, Hillel, one of the first Talmudic sages, together with the Sanhedrin, decreed the granting of an emergency Pruzbul, or special writ, granting extension beyond the six-year period. (Pruzbul comes from the Greek, meaning "from before the Council.")

There are provisions in the Torah for help for the poor and for the humane treatment of beasts of burden. These are among the first laws of this nature ever enacted.

The word "slave" does not occur in the Torah. It is interesting to note that there is no such word in the Hebrew dictionary. The only word used is Oved or Eved, from the Hebrew Avodah, which means "work." A slave was considered a worker with the basic rights of a human being.

The Torah establishes clearly the rights of women as to ownership of private property, when no male heir is present. This precept was handed down to Moses in the case of Zelophechad's daughters who claimed their father's property. God commanded that this be granted them. It was stipulated, however, that they marry within their own tribe so as not to increase the land-ownership of tribes out of proportion.

The Torah also establishes the rights of women in the home and in family life. By instituting the Kethuba or Writ of Alimony to protect a woman against an unscrupulous husband, it further clearly defines the rules and laws of marriage. It definitely proclaims the full rights of women not only at home but as public leaders. When we remember that equality of the sexes is a relatively new concept in our modern day world, we can appreciate more fully the greatness of these laws.

NATIONAL CONSCIOUSNESS

The Torah commands every Jew to visit the Temple in Jerusalem three times a year: on Sukkoth, Passover and Shavuoth. This is why these three holidays are called in Hebrew, "The Shalosh Regalim" from the Hebrew "Regel" meaning "foot." (Most Jews traveled on foot when visiting the Holy Temple.) This directive was aimed at keeping every Jew politically, cosmopolitically, religiously and educationally well informed. It later helped preserve the Jewish nation during the years of Exile, where the houses of worship substituted for the Temple in Jerusalem. Wherever there were Jews, they made their houses of worship, houses of gathering and study. The Jews called their Synagogues and Temples, Beth Tefilah "house of prayer," Beth Hamidrash, "house of study," and Beth Knesseth, "house of gathering." (The Israeli parliament is called the Knesseth.) No wonder the Founding Fathers took the Bible as their model in establishing the Constitution of the United States along the lines of the teaching of Moses.

SPIRITUAL SECURITY

Moses, realizing that religion is spiritual security for a united family and national life, introduced the worship of one God according to the directives of the Torah. He established a central place of worship, the Tabernacle, which was later replaced in Israel with the Temple. He regulated the order of service and sacrifice which, after the destruction of the Temple, was superseded by prayers.

Moses appointed Aaron, his brother, as the Kohen Gadol (high priest). Aaron, fitted for high office by dint of prior achievements, sterling character, education and qualities of spiritual leadership, was selected by God. Moses' appointment of his brother therefore, held no tinge of favoritism or self-interest.

The Levites were appointed as assistants to Aaron by virtue of the fact that they had not been slaves in Egypt, but overseers and supervisers. Thus they have had the opportunity to become the most educated and spiritual-minded section of the Jewish people.

RELIGIOUS DOGMA

The dogma of Jewish Religion is clearly expressed and summarized in the following three sources:

IN THE PARAGRAPH "SHMA" of Deuteronomy it is written: "Hear O Israel, the Lord our God, the Lord is one." Complete belief is expressed in one God as the single power controlling the whole universe. We are told therefore:

1. To love our God with all our heart, and with all our soul and with all our might.
2. To teach the words of God to our children.
3. In order to remember the words of God, it is directed to bind them on the arm, to place them as frontlets between the eyes, and write them on the door posts. We therefore fasten a Mezuza on the doorposts of our homes. The Mezuza is a metal container in which we put a parchment scroll on which there are hand-

written two sections of the portion of the Shema. (Mezuza in Hebrew means "doorpost.")

IN THE TEN COMMANDMENTS There, the existence of one God is emphasized and the relationship of man to God, and man to man developed. They are as follows:

1. I am the Lord thy God which brought thee out of Egypt.
2. Thou shall not make thee any graven image.
3. Thou shall not take the name of the Lord in vain.
4. Keep the Sabbath day to sanctify it.
5. Honor thy father and thy mother.
6. Thou shall not kill.
7. Thou shall not commit adultery.
8. Thou shall not steal.
9. Thou shall not bear false witness against thy neighbor.
10. Thou shall not desire thy neighbor's wife nor anything that is thy neighbor's.

IN THE THIRTEEN ARTICLES OF FAITH, as written by Maimonides.

ESSENCE OF THE TORAH

It was Hillel, who, when challenged to state the essence of the Torah in one sentence, expressed it thus: "Do not do unto your neighbor that which is abhorrent or unpleasant to yourself." The rest of the Torah he maintained, was merely commentary.

PHILOSOPHY OF THE TORAH

In Deuteronomy, the portion of "Re'eh" is devoted to the principle of man's free choice to do good or evil. The Talmudic sage, Rabbi Akiba, held that while religion is based on predestination and everything in human life is fore-ordained, God gives to man the privilege of free choice. A choice, that is, either beneficially to influence his life and future, or to follow the path of chaos, destruction and oblivion.

God created all people equal with an equal opportunity to be either good or bad. If he had created all people good, there would be no opportunity for man to develop his mind and character, and man would have remained in a low animal state of mind.

The Hebrew sages have specifically advised that Repentance, Prayer and Charity can positively alter man's existence. In this connection, God has designated the mountains Gerizim and Ebal, as symbols (Deuteronomy). They stand as immutable reminders of this free, democratic choice.

Deuteronomy also contains God's command to count off the forty-nine days of the Omer (*see* Holidays, Passover). There is a very interesting and important reason for this counting off. In that way God wanted to impress upon the people that time is relative and must be used with proper care. The lifetime of a butterfly is infinitesimal compared to that of man; and man's life span is but a millionth of a second, astronomically speaking. Precious time, then, is irretrievably lost, unless it is spent in doing good.

RELIGION AND MENTAL HEALTH

Religion stimulates many salutary conditions. It brings relaxation and rest, freedom from worry and tension; it organizes the forces of the mind, and brings trust in a strong God in one's hour of need. These are much sought-after attitudes in the practice of modern psychiatry. Religion also supplies both immediate and long-range motivations. Thousands of years ago there was a god or image for every one of man's deeds, desires, whims and anxieties. But from the days of the Patriarch Abraham, belief, faith and dependence upon one God have led to concentration in prayer—concentration, that is, on the sincerity, quality and earnest purposefulness of one's praying, not on the expert and routine rendition of a particular set of prayers. Such a concept strengthens the idea of freedom of choice and reinforces individual integrity and human dignity. Through the mind one may choose his fate and help to control his destiny. It is interesting to note that these beneficial influences were grasped at primarily by the poor and overworked. It is for this reason that holidays exert such a salutary effect upon mind and body.

Hebrew sages promised happiness by encouraging the Jews to see only good in people, and by meeting one another with smiles and kind words. The sages abjured black magic and fortune-telling. It is plain to see that here we have the fundamentals of modern psychology, psychosomatic medicine and mental hygiene. Here, very clearly articulated, is the idea that mental relaxation and rest result in physical rest and well-being, that a healthy mind develops a healthy body. This is the present-day motto of the Israeli Chalutzim (pioneers).

According to the Bible and other religious writings, God is omnipresent. He exists everywhere, and in every human being, is identified with the soul. In this way Godliness becomes goodness in man.

Although religion teaches that all is pre-ordained, the Torah repeatedly encourages man, through its precepts, to channelize his talents and abilities—positively, constructively

135

and creatively. In this way is leadership, scholarship and wisdom developed. This of necessity accrues to the betterment of mankind on earth. Eminent examples of this can be seen in the deeds and teachings of leaders and sages such as Moses, Rabbi Akiba, Maimonides and others. (*See* section on Sages and Leaders.)

NEVIIM (*Prophets, or second part of Tanach*)

Following is the general order of most of the books of the Prophets:

JOSHUA, covering the conquest of the land of Canaan.

JUDGES, covering the 200-year period during which the tribes were ruled independently by their judges.

SAMUEL, BOOK ONE, includes Eli, Samuel, King Saul and King David.

SAMUEL, BOOK TWO, includes King David and his sons.

KINGS, BOOK ONE, story of Solomon and succeeding kings of Israel and Judea, and the prophet Elijah.

KINGS, BOOK TWO, activities of the prophet Elisha and the kings who ruled Israel and Judea just before the destruction of the first Temple.

THE RECORDED SERMONS AND PROPHECIES of Isaiah, Jeremiah, Ezekiel, Hosea, Joel, Amos, Obadiah, Jonah, Micah, Nahum, Habakkuk, Zephaniah, Hagai, Zechariah, Malachi.

KETUVIM OR HAGIOGRAPHA (*third part of Tanach*)

The Ketuvim consist of the following books:

PSALMS

PROVERBS OF SOLOMON

LAMENTATIONS OF JOB

SONG OF SONGS, by Solomon

SCROLL OF RUTH

SCROLL OF EICHA, by the Prophet Jeremiah, describing the destruction of Jerusalem

KOHELETH or ECCLESIASTES, words of wisdom by King Solomon

SCROLL OF ESTHER, the story of Purim

DANIEL, the story of the Prophet Daniel

EZRA, the story of Ezra the Scribe

NEHEMIAH, the story of Nehemiah

CHRONICLES, BOOKS ONE AND TWO, a brief history from Adam to Cyrus, king of Persia

EXTRA WRITINGS (*of the post-Tanach period during the second Temple*)

These contain the Apocrypha and the Apocalypse.

THE APOCRYPHA

consists of the following books:

THE THIRD BOOK OF EZRA, which tells the story of Zerubabel, of the house of David, who received permission from King Darius to visit Judea, as the victor's reward in a debate between the king's pages as to what is the strongest thing on earth. His argument was that women are the strongest.

MACCABEES: BOOK ONE, tells the story of the Jews from the time of Antioches Epiphanes until the death of Simon Maccabee.

MACCABEES: BOOK TWO, from Seleucus IV to the death of Nicanor.

MACCABEES: BOOK THREE, God's punishment of Ptolemy IV, for polluting the sanctuary of the Temple.

THE BOOK OF TOBIT, the miracle story of a man named Tobit and his son Tobias.

THE BOOK OF JUDITH, tells of the courage and heroism of Judith in eliminating General Holofernes.

BEL AND THE DRAGON, relating the story of Daniel who fought the idol Bel and the mythical god Dragon. The story also tells of how Daniel tamed the ferocious and hungry lions when thrown into their den.

SUSANNA, who was falsely accused of adultery by the elders, but was finally vindicated.

SPECIAL ADDITION TO THE SCROLL OF ESTHER.

SONG OF THE THREE CHILDREN, the story of Azarias, Chanamia and Mishoel, who were saved from death in a furnace.

PRAYER OF MANASSEH, who was the king of Judea and the son of Hezekiah.

THE BOOK OF BARUCH, a book of wisdom written by Baruch, the secretary of the Prophet Jeremiah.

EPISTLE OF JEREMIAH, in which Jeremiah warns the Exiles against worshipping idols.

WISDOM OF BEN SIRAH, a book written by Ben Sirah, who is widely quoted by Talmudic sages. It contains words of wisdom about religion; relationship to parents, friends and society; steadfastness of character and behavior toward tyrants; freedom of individual action; relationship to God; carefulness of speech; evil of foolishness, anger and quarrel; women; greediness; education, poverty, riches, feasts, songs, prayer, life and death; and a short sketch of Jewish history.

WISDOM OF SOLOMON, a philosophical book concerning God, written by an unknown author.

MACCABEES: BOOK IV, a book of stoicism.

THE APOCALYPSE

consists of the following books:

BOOK OF ENOCH, Enoch, the father of Methuselah, is thought to be the author. It discusses God as supreme judge, contains a history of sin, parables, discourses in astronomy, etc.

BOOK OF JUBILEE, authors unknown. It is the first attempt at Midrash or folklore, beginning with Adam.

TESTAMENTS OF TWELVE PATRIARCHS, Testaments of the twelve sons of Jacob.

PSALMS OF SOLOMON, a collection of eighteen Psalms in which the Sadducees and last Maccabean princes are denounced. Its author is thought to have been a member of the Pharisees.

APOCALYPSE OF BARUCH, describes visions of Baruch, the secretary of Jeremiah, concerning Resurrection and the Messiah.

EZRA: BOOK IV, deals with Ezra's bitter complaints of the fate of Israel.

ASSUMPTION OF MOSES, an address by Moses to Joshua before he died.

BOOK OF ADAM AND EVE, which contains legends concerning Adam and Eve and their descendants.

SIBYLLINE ORACLES, prophecies of several prophetesses called Sibyls.

THE TALMUD (*Oral law*)

These are the books of Jewish civil and religious law (500 B.C.E.—500 C.E.). The Talmud contains:

1. THE MISHNA, which is an interpretation and addition to the Torah.

2. THE GEMARA, which is an interpretation and addition to the Torah and Mishna.

3. TOSEFTA (additions), laws not included in the Halacha (law) section of the Talmud. Compiled by Rabbi Nehemiah, pupil of Rabbi Akiba, first compiler of the Mishna.

4. BRAITHOTH (external statements by Sages) omitted in the Mishna but quoted in the Gemara.

5. FOURTEEN ADDITIONAL EXTRA CANONICAL TRACTATES.

6. DISCOURSES in Medicine, History, Philosophy, Ethics, Astronomy, Science, Mysticism, Agronomy, Mathematics, etc.

7. AGADA, legends and folklore.

THE MISHNA (*from Hebrew—meaning to study. Compiled in 219 C.E.*)

The Mishna was composed in Hebrew by the Tanaim (students and teachers) and is divided into sections or orders. Each order is divided into tractates; each tractate, into chapters; each chapter into small studies called Mishnas.

These are the orders:

1. ZERAIM, laws concerning land cultivation, duties of land owners, donations to priests, prayers and blessings. (11 tractates)

2. MOED, laws concerning holidays. (12 tractates)

3. NASHIM, laws concerning marriage, divorce and family life. (7 tractates)

4. NEZIKIN, civil and criminal laws, and regulations relating to damages, accidents, penalties, etc. (10 tractates)

5. KODSHIM, sacrifices and dietary observances. (11 tractates)
6. TAHAROTH, laws concerning personal cleanliness. (12
   tractates)

The Mishna was edited by Rabbi Judah, Hanasi (the
Prince). Up to his time, all debates of the Tanaim were
either written down by their pupils or passed on from mouth
to mouth. Rabbi Judah gathered all the debates and decisions
of the preceding Tanaim and put them together into one
book, the Mishna. With each law, Rabbi Judah included all
controversial opinions, in order to give scholars a chance to
study all points of view on each question. The following are
examples of three mishnas:

1. Order of Nezikin, Tractate of Baba Kama, Chapter
Eight, Mishna One: He who injures his neighbor must pay
compensation for damage, for pain, for medical expenses, for
loss of time from work, and for insult. How should the damage be determined?

If a person is blinded or crippled by another, he is to be
appraised as if he were offered in the slave market before his
injury, and the compensation should be calculated on that
appraisal.

Pain: If a person hurts another with a hot spit or with a
pin or with his nail, and makes a wound, he should pay as
compensation what a man of his kind would accept to suffer
such pain.

Healing: If a man hurts another, he must heal him. If
ulcers grow because of the injury, he has to pay as many
times as the wound opens again after healing. He must pay
for the healing.

For loss of time: Estimated as though the victim were a watchman of cucumbers and were paid the damage for the loss of a hand or leg.

Insult: Estimated by respective status of the persons involved. It is an insult that calls for compensation if the insulted person is nude, blind, or asleep. If a sleeping person offends another, he is not liable. If in a fall from a roof he injured and insulted another, he must pay for damages but not for the insult, since there was no offensive intention.

2. Order of Nezikin, Baba Metzia, Chapter One, Mishna Three: If a man riding on an animal saw an article and said to another, "Give it to me," and the latter picked it up and said, "I have picked it up for myself," the article belongs to him. But if he gave it first to the rider and then said, "I have picked it up for myself," his claim will not be allowed.

3. Order of Nezikin, Tractate Baba Bathra, Chapter Nine, Mishna Ten: If a house fell on a man and his mother, both the schools of Hillel and of Shammai agree that the estate should be divided equally among the heirs of the mother and the son. Rabbi Akiba said, "I hold that the estate should be left in the hands of those who occupy them." Ben Azai said to him, "We feel sorry over divided opinions on other subjects, and you come along and bring forth a division on things about which both the schools of Hillel and of Shammai agree."

Commentaries, interpretations and debates follow each Mishna by the Sages of Gemara (the Amoraim), who interpret the ideas of the Tanaim (Sages of the Mishna). Commentaries of later sages like Rashi, Tosafists, etc., interpret the ideas, debates and reasons for those debates, of both the Tanaim and Amoraim.

THE GEMARA (*from the Aramaic meaning, to study. Compiled in 500 C.E.*)

The Gemara was written by the Amoraim (interpreters) and edited by Rav Ashi and later by Ravinah. While the Mishna was written in Hebrew, the Gemara was written mostly in Aramaic, which is linguistically related to Hebrew, and was the language spoken by the Jews at that time.

Decisions as to meaning and shades of meanings in both the Mishna and the Gemara, were arrived at through debate. The majority opinion prevailed. Recorded along with the debates, were wise sayings, stories with a moral, fables and the like. These are incorporated in the Talmud as the Agada or legends and stories. The stories were told by the sages between debates, as a means of relaxation. These sages were the first creators of Jewish folklore, which continued through the ages. There were the folk stories about Elijah the prophet; Rabbi Loew of Bohemia (16th Century), who created the Golem (robot); the stories about the great Hasidic rabbis of the 18th and 19th Centuries; the folk wits, Hershele Ostropoler and Motke Habad; the people of Chelm; and many others.

These stories reflected Jewish life and folkways of their day—the customs, ceremonies, superstitions, teachings and humor. The following are examples of Talmudic and Midrashic tales:

1. A father and son were traveling to a distant town. The father rode on the donkey and the son followed. When the people of one village scolded the father for letting the boy walk while he rode, he got off and put his son on the donkey. At the next town the people scolded the boy for letting his old father walk, so father and son both mounted

143

the donkey. They were then scolded for making the poor donkey carry such a heavy load. They then tried walking beside the donkey, but the people laughed and said, "There go three asses, why does not one ride on the other?" The father and son finally picked up the donkey and carried it. The simple moral—one must not try to satisfy everyone.

2. Another Agada tale runs as follows: A servant brought back from the market a fish which was not fresh. His master said to him, "Choose one of three punishments: either pay me fifty shekels, receive fifty lashes, or eat the fish." The servant chose to eat the fish. Halfway through, he got too sick to finish, so he chose the fifty lashes instead. Halfway through the beating, he could stand the pain no longer and begged for the privilege of paying the fifty shekel fine. The moral here is: "A greedy man is often a foolish man"; or: "The easiest way out may very well be the worst." (Mechilta)

3. A king had a beautiful orchard of rare fruit. He set two watchmen to guard it. One was blind, the other lame. Said the lame to the blind: "Put me on your shoulders and we both will enjoy the exotic fruit every day." Later, when the king came for the fruit, he found none. When he asked the watchmen what had happened to the fruits, the blind man said, "Do I have eyes to see them?" The lame man said, "Do I have feet to walk?" Then the king put the lame man on top of the blind and punished them as one. (Tractate Sanhedrin)

4. A blind man walked in the night holding a torch. When asked why he held the torch, since he could not see, he replied, "People will see *me* and will save me from dangers." (Tractate Megila)

5. A man had two wives, a young one and an old one. The young one pulled his gray hair out, and the old one, his dark hair. He ended by being completely bald. (Tractate Baba Kama)

6. A fox, walking on the bank of a river, saw some fish in the water. He asked them, "Why do you run from place to place?" They answered, "We are running from the nets, spread by humans." So the fox said to them, "How about coming up on the ground and I'll protect you, as my grandfather protected your grandfathers, who lived peacefully together." The fish answered: "We have been told that you are the smartest of all animals and beasts but now we see that you are very foolish. If we have to fear for our lives in water, we should certainly be in peril where there is no water, and where we should be sure to die." (Tractate Berachot. This parable was used by Rabbi Joshua in answer to a Roman matron.)

7. Emperor Hadrian's daughter, remarking on the homeliness of Rabbi Joshua, son of Hanania, said, "So much beautiful knowledge in such an ugly vessel!" Rabbi Joshua asked her, "In what kind of vessels do you keep wine?" "In earthen vessels, of course," she answered. "Why don't you keep your wine in gold vessels as befits a Roman emperor's daughter?" he asked. She ordered the wine in the palace to be put in gold vessels.

When Emperor Hadrian tasted the wine it was sour. His daughter then told him about Rabbi Joshua's advice. When he asked Rabbi Joshua why he had caused the spoilage of his wine, Rabbi Joshua recounted to him the entire conversation. Hadrian then asked, "Aren't there handsome men who are also clever and learned?" "If these same men had been ugly," replied Rabbi Joshua, "they would have been cleverer and more learned." (Tractate Nedarim)

There are two Talmuds, the Babylonian Talmud and the Jerusalem Talmud. The Babylonian Talmud is more popular since it is more explanatory, having more commentaries and a more detailed explanation.

SPIRITUAL ESSENCE OR PHILOSOPHY OF THE TALMUD

The Torah and the sages of the Talmud gave very clear expression to the relationship of man to God and man to man. In the Ten Commandments the first five deal with man's relationship to God and the rest with man's relation to man. In their sermons the Prophets constantly reminded the Jews, and the other nations as well, that there is only one God in the world and only He should be served. They warned against corruption and against other mistreatment of their fellow men. The Torah and the Prophets, and the sages of the Talmud after them, always counselled the people to be pure of heart and mind. God commanded them to wear a Talis and Tefilin as symbols of purity of heart and soul.

The Talmudic sages taught that there are many dividends as reward for good living that man can earn and enjoy on earth. But the principal from which these dividends are derived will be served to man in the hereafter, or world to come. It is earned by the following deeds:

1. Honoring one's father and mother.
2. The practice of charity.
3. Timely attendance at the house of study.
4. Hospitality to wayfarers.
5. Visiting the sick.

6. Providing dowries for poor brides.
7. Attending the dead to the grave.
8. Devotion in prayer.
9. Acting as peacemaker.
10. The study of the Torah which outweighs the rest combined.

POST-TALMUDIC LITERATURE

1. POST GEMARA MIDRASH (folklore in sermonic form). Fourteen volumes.
2. RESPONSA (answers to Religious dogmatic questions) given by sages beginning with Shisna Gaon (670 C.E.), and continuing through the centuries.
3. BOOKS OF CODES, beginning with Sheiltoth (questions) by Achai Gaon (760 C.E.) followed by the Alfes Code, the Code of Maimonides, the four Turim (rows), a compendium by Rabbi Jacob, the Shulchan Aruch, a condensation of the four Turim; and other Codes, unto our time.
4. BOOKS ON PHILOSOPHY, GRAMMAR, HISTORY, POETRY, PROSE, TRAVEL, MYSTICISM, SCIENCE, ETC. Thousands of works by Talmudic and post-Talmudic sages through the Middle Ages.

THE SHULCHAN ARUCH

The words "Shulchan Aruch" mean a prepared table. When the laws of the Talmud became so complicated that many people, including scholars, had difficulty in understanding it, Rabbi Joseph Karo, the 16th Century sage, summarized the laws of the Talmud in a concise and simple form, entering the final decisions of the sages and omitting the debates. The

Shulchan Aruch, following the order of the Code of the four Turim (published in 1340 C.E.), is divided into four parts:

1. ORACH CHAIM: on personal habits and relationship to God.
2. YOREH DE'AH: on dietary laws.
3. EBEN HA'EZER: on family relationships.
4. CHOSHEN MISHPAT: on monetary questions, damages, etc.

CULTURE DURING THE MIDDLE AGES

Part of the Talmud can be considered as Jewish literature of the Middle Ages because it was compiled about 500 C.E. After the appearance of the Talmud, the writings of the Saburaim followed. Then came the writings and interpretations of the Gaonim. (Gaon is a special term for rabbi, which indicates that he has authority in the community. Literally, it means genius.) The best known of the Gaonim was Saadia Gaon. In addition to winning a controversy with the Karaite sect, he wrote excellent interpretations of the Talmud, also books in Arabic and in Greek for the purpose of introducing Jewish literature and ethics to the non-Jewish world.

During the Spanish Golden Era (900-1200 C.E.) which followed the Gaoni period, there appeared men like Maimonides, Ibn Gabirol, Ibn Ezra, Judah Halevi and many others who enriched Jewish and world culture. They won recognition also in the non-Jewish world.

During the Middle Ages, cultural activities of European nations were restricted almost completely to monks. Jewish culture, on the other hand, had a universal and cosmopolitical character. It was created by many Jewish scholars of many lands. Learning was highly prized by Jews. Every Jewish child was taught to read and write, and the man of learning was the most highly respected member of the community.

THE SIDDUR

The Siddur contains all daily and weekly prayers. The word comes from "Seder," which in Hebrew means order. The Siddur contains all prayers in a special sequence. The daily prayers are found in the beginning of the book. The Sabbath prayers, which are said once a week, are found in the middle of the book. At the end of the book we find prayers for some of the annual holidays.

The most successful compilations of prayers were those of Rabban Gamaliel, Rabbi Akiba, Rav Amram Gaon (856 C.E.) and Saadia Gaon. The Siddurs in use at present were arranged during the last centuries. One, the Ashkenazic version is used mainly by Misnagdim; the other, the Sephard Siddur, which has some slight variations, is used by the Hasidim. Currently, there are undertakings by the Conservative and Reform groups in Jewish religious life, to revise the official Siddur still further. The Siddur contains:

1. Portions from the Torah.
2. Sections of the Talmud.
3. Psalms of David and Solomon.
4. Prayers written by the sages, such as "Lecha Dodi," a song written by Solomon Alkabetz and many other poems.
5. The thirteen Articles of Faith written by Maimonides.
6. Special blessings recited when lighting candles, eating, drinking, washing hands, etc.

7. Some individual, historical, national and universal prayers.

THE MACHZOR

The Machzor is a special compilation of prayers arranged in two volumes. One contains all the prayers for services on Rosh Hashanah and Yom Kippur; the other, detailed services for Passover, Sukkoth and Shavuoth.

CHAPTER NINE

WISDOM OF THE TALMUD

In the previous chapter, we discussed the Talmud, its origin, and its significant place in Jewish culture. We also pointed out that the Agada section of the Talmud contains wise sayings which have guided generations of Jewish people in their relationships between man and God, man and his family, and man and fellow man. Below is a representative, but by no means complete selection of the wisdom of the Talmud.

In most cases, the source of the selection is indicated by the name of the tractate.

PART ONE   *Man to God, and Man to Man*

God prefers the heart (Sanhedrin).

You do not pass a law which the majority of people could not observe (Baba Kama).

Loose talk leads to sin (Abot).

Avoid anger and you will avoid sin (Berachot).

By three things a man's character is recognized: by his cup, by his anger, and by his pocket (Eruvin).

In argument, he who stops first is the more cultured one (Kidushin).

Why was Man created last? To be reminded, if he becomes haughty, that a mosquito came before him (Sanhedrin).

A small coin in an empty vessel makes the most noise (Baba Metzia).

He who sustains a loss should not be told of it while sick. He may lose his mind also.

A man is born with closed hands: he expects to grab the whole world; he dies with open hands: he takes nothing with him.

A human being is here today—in the grave tomorrow (Berachot).

A man's mind should always incline toward his fellow men (Ketubot).

Be friendly with every man in whatever station; each man has a favorable hour (Pesachim).

The punishment of a liar is—not to be believed when he tells the truth (Sanhedrin).

What city is considered big? The one which contains ten idle people.

God has given more wisdom to a woman than to a man (Nida).

False hatred brings quarrel in his home (Sabbath).

A court decision which the majority of people do not accept is not considered legal (Yerushalmi Sabbath).

Custom nullifies law (Yerushalmi Yebamot).

Rivalry among students increases knowledge (Baba Bathra).

One who commits a crime as an agent, is also a criminal (Baba Kama).

Pious men are considered greater than angels (Sanhedrin).

Chew with your teeth and you'll find strength in your feet (Sabbath).

He who cures for nothing, is worth nothing (Baba Kama).

He who depends upon his wife's earnings will never succeed in life (Pesachim).

He who buys something, finds something; he who sells something, loses something (Baba Metzia).

He who insults a fellow man in public is like a murderer (Baba Metzia).

He who prays for his friend is answered first (Baba Kama).

It is not the mouse that is the thief, but the hole (Gitin).

Charity is more important than all commandments put together (Baba Bathra).

The Lord hates him who talks one way and thinks another (Pesachim).

Even a thief prays to God that he shall succeed (Berachot).

He who runs after greatness—greatness runs away from him (Eruvin).

Cash in hand is the best bargainer (Baba Metzia).

The grapes should pray for the leaves; if not for the leaves there would be no grapes (Chulin).

By his compliments could a person be recognized (Berachot).

Let your ears hear what your mouth says (Berachot).

Silence is good for the learned—all the more for fools (Pesachim).

There are those to whom money is more important than their own body (Berachot).

Everything God does is for the best (Berachot).

The greater the man the more dangerous his vices (Sukkah).

He who adds too much—subtracts (Sanhedrin).

Rabbi Isaac said: "If a man says, 'I have tried hard and did not succeed,' do not believe him. If he says, 'I did not try hard and succeeded,' do not believe him, but if he says, 'I have tried hard and succeeded,' believe him."

There is neither first nor last in the Torah (Pesachim).

A person dreams about what he thinks when awake (Berachot).

He who studies his lesson one hundred times is not equal to him who studies one hundred and one times (Hagiga).

On the sandy seashore, a bush is considered a cedar of
Lebanon (Pesachim).

Do not mourn tomorrow's sorrow today (Yebamot).

If you leave Torah study for a day, it will leave you for two
days (Yerushalmi Berachot).

Two dogs can kill a lion (Sanhedrin).

Worry kills the strongest man (Sanhedrin).

To an old man a small hill becomes a mountain (Sabbath).

A good deed is greater than alms (Sukkah).

To receive strangers is greater than receiving God (Sabbath).

Value the drink of wine when it draws strangers into har-
mony (Sanhedrin).

Worry about present troubles, not about future troubles; they
may never come (Berachot).

The ignoramus jumps first (Megila).

Everything is in the hands of God except fear of God
(Berachot).

He who is busy observing one commandment, is excused from
another (Sukkah).

I have learned much from my teachers, more from my friends
but most from my pupils (Taanit).

If an ignorant person is too pious, avoid him (Sabbath).

If a man says, "With what shall I eat this bread," take it
away from him. He is not hungry (Sanhedrin).

Some people eat, while others have to say grace (Berachot).

Even when a sword is upon the neck of a person, he should
not lose hope of help from Heaven (Berachot).

The dwarf who becomes a high official, becomes a tall man
(Rosh Hashanah).

Two kings cannot wear one crown (Chulin).

It is better for a woman to love a young cripple than a rich
old man.

Love without scolding is not love.

It is easier to acquire an enemy than a friend.

Crows love each other (Pesachim).

A man has three true friends: his family, his money and his good deeds.

Do not say, "I like educated people only." You must love all people.

In times of prosperity, all men act like brothers.

Three men get no answer to their prayers: he who lends money without witnesses or security; he who subjects himself to a master, and he who lets his wife lord over him.

God forgives a forced deed (Nedarim).

For a guest to invite another guest is bad manners.

A man should spend less than he has on food, as much as he has on clothes, and more than he has on his wife and children (Chulin).

On account of a small quarrel, Jerusalem was destroyed (Gitin).

On account of a broken axle, the city of Bethar was destroyed (Gitin).

On account of a chicken, the city of Tur Malka was destroyed (Gitin).

Lucky is the generation in which the great listen to the small (Rosh Hashanah).

Jealousy brings women more pain than thorns (Yebamot).

A man is jealous of everybody except his son and pupil (Sanhedrin).

He to whom a miracle occurred never knows that it has occurred (Nida).

Do not worry about what will happen after you are gone (Sanhedrin).

A house is blessed when each helps the other (Ketubot).

A judgment postponed is a judgment nullified (Sanhedrin).

He who steals from a thief, enjoys the stealing (Berachot).

Poverty follows the poor (Baba Kama).

A liar recognizes a liar (Avodah Zarah).

Marry a wife below you, seek a friend above you (Yebamot).

Wine in, secret out (Eruvin).

Ten measures of talk were sent down from Heaven; women took nine (Kidushin).

A pot belonging to two partners is neither warm nor cold (Eruvin).

Sixty men ran after a man who had a good breakfast in the morning, and could not catch him (Baba Kama).

A quarrel in a home is like a worm in an onion (Sota).

No man can testify against himself (Ketubot).

No man considers himself wicked (Sanhedrin).

No man lifts his little finger unless it was foreordained in Heaven (Chulin).

No man should be held responsible for words spoken in grief (Baba Bathra).

A lion roars when he is satisfied—a man sins when he has plenty (Berachot).

An imprisoned man cannot free himself alone (Berachot).

Peace brings prosperity (Yerushalmi Ukzin).

Only a fast moving man can be urged to move fast (Makkot).

Where there is food, friends swarm at the gates; but at the prison gates, they are absent (Sabbath).

For the refined, the flute makes music; for the boors it only produces noise (Yoma).

A man prefers the little that is his own to the much which is his friend's (Baba Metzia).

To a man in anger, God himself is not important (Nedarim).

156

Roast your meat while the fire is burning (Sanhedrin).

No place is too small for lovers (Baba Metzia).

Death is preferred to being alone (Taanit).

Honor your doctor so as not to need him (Yerushalmi Taanit).

If a thing is fit for you, it will not get away from you.

A sword and a book do not mix (Avoda Zara).

A man may feel what his eyes do not see (Megila).

The elephant fears the mosquito (Sabbath).

A man does not sin for another's sake (Baba Metzia).

PIRKE ABOT

The following are sayings in the tractate of Pirke Abot (Ethics of the Fathers) of the order of Nezikin.

Judah, the son of Tabbai, says, "In the Judge's offices, be impartial."

Simon the Just: "The world rests upon three things—the Torah, service to God and good deeds."

Jose, the son of Johanan: "Let thy house be open to the poor."

Nittai the Arbelite: "Keep away from bad neighbors."

Rabbi Judah: "Know what is above you, a seeing eye and a hearing ear."

Rabbi Gamaliel: "Excellent is the study of the Torah when combined with work. Study without work leads to sin."

Hillel: "Do not do unto others what you would not wish others to do unto you. Love thy friend as thyself."

Shemaiah: "Love work and hate lordship."

Rabbi Chanina: "He whose work exceeds wisdom, his wisdom will endure."

Hillel, the second: "If I will not do it myself, who will do it for me? If I am only for myself, what am I? And if I do not do it now, when?"

Rabbi Ishmael: "Be affable to the young."

Rabbi Akiba: "Everything is predetermined, yet free will is granted."

Rabbi Zoma: "He is wise who learns from all men; he is strong who controls his temper; he is rich who rejoices in his portion; he is honored who honors others."

Nittai the Arbelite: "Abandon not the belief in retribution."

Shemayah: "Hate tyrrany."

Hillel: "Be the disciple of Aaron, loving peace, loving his fellow men."

Rabban Simon: "By three things is the world preserved: by truth, justice and peace."

Rabbi Judah the Prince: "All deeds are recorded."

Hillel: "Do not separate thyself from the congregation, and trust not in thyself until one day before death. Also, judge not thy neighbor until thou art in his place."

"An empty-headed man can not be sin-fearing, an ignorant person pious, a shame-faced one learned, an ill-tempered man a teacher. In places where there are no men, strive to be a man."

Rabbi Mathiah: "Be beforehand in greeting people, and rather be a tail to a lion than a head to a fox."

Rabbi Meir: "Look not at the flask, but at what is inside."

Samuel: "Do not rejoice when your enemy falls, lest the Lord see it and it displease him."

Rabbi Joshua: "An evil eye, evil inclination and hatred of people put a man out of this world."

Rabbi Jose: "Let your friend's property be important to you as your own."

Rabbi Chanina: "Pray for the welfare of the Government."

Rabbi Chanina ben Dosa: "He whom the people like, the Lord likes also."

Rabbi Elazar: "Where there is no knowledge, there are no good manners."

Shammai: "Receive people with a smile."

PART TWO *Relationship of Husband and Wife, Parent and Child*

Happy is the husband of a good wife (Yebamot).

A man gets a wife in accordance with his deeds.

Said Rav: "He who marries for money, shall be disappointed in his children" (Kidushin).

A woman has real contentment only in her husband's home.

If your wife is short, bend down and whisper into her ear (Baba Bathra).

No man should marry with the thought of later divorcing his wife (Yebamot).

Let no man drink from one glass, and put his eyes upon another glass (Nedarim).

Men usually follow the advice of women.

A woman should never sit idle in her home (Yerushalmi Ketubot).

A woman was created for beauty, for beautiful clothes and for children (Ketubot).

A woman is more modest than a man (Ketubot).

A woman will always uncover the dish to know what her friend is cooking (Tosefta Taharot).

A good woman is a treasure to her husband (Ben Sira).

Idleness brings melancholy (Ketubot).

Is he a father who hates his son? (Sanhedrin).

Is he a father who would testify against his son? (Avoda Zara).

Pity the father who has exiled his children (Berachot).

An infant misses his father (Sabbath).

A father should teach his son a profession. Some say—also to swim (Kidushin).

A son can be forced to support his father (Yerushalmi Nedarim).

Sons resemble their mother's brothers (Ketubot).

No man can exist without a wife and no woman without a husband (Yerushalmi Berachot).

A man should build a house and plant a vineyard before he marries.

The man should seek a wife but not the woman a husband.

An unmarried Jew is not considered a whole human being (Yebamot).

A man who has no wife, has no joy, no blessing, no peace of mind (Yebamot).

His wife is like his own body (Berachot).

A husband should always be careful of his wife's honor because the welfare of the home depends upon her (Baba Metzia).

A wife demands with her heart, a husband with his mouth (Eruvin).

His wife is his home.

If a man is poor, let him support his daughters and have his sons go and beg (Ketubot).

An adult daughter should not spoil her looks while mourning for her father (Taanit).

Grandchildren are like children (Yebamot).

A man should call his son-in-law—son, and his daughter-in-law—daughter.

A father who signs away his property to his sons while still alive sets masters over himself (Baba Metzia).

He who has a bad wife shall not inherit Purgatory (Eruvin).

To divorce a bad wife, is considered a good deed (Yebamot).

Rabbi Simon, the son of Gamaliel, says, "I praise the children of the East because they kiss only the hand, not the mouth."

Be amiable and modest before all people, but most of all in your household.

He who raises the child is called the father, not he who merely causes his birth.

Look at the bridegroom as at a king.

You have the right to disqualify yourself, but not your son (Yebamot).

To marry one's daughter to a boor is like tying her and throwing her to a tiger (Pesachim).

A woman seeks marriage more than the man (Yebamot).

The Lord has equalized the duties of man and woman (Baba Kama).

Women are a nation by themselves (Sabbath).

A clever son understands a wink; a fool only a fist.

He who hopes that his wife will die first and that he will inherit from her, usually is buried first (Tosefta Sota).

A father pities his son, his son pities his children (Sota).

A man should learn a trade, then God will provide for him.

He who marries a wife should first inspect her brothers.

She is a bad wife who sets his table, then curses him or refuses to eat with him (Yebamot).

A husband should take care not to make his wife cry; women cry easily and God's punishment is swift (Baba Metzia).

A bad wife is like leprosy, let the husband divorce her and be cured (Yebamot).

A child who talks in the street, repeats either his father's or
his mother's words (Sukkah).

A child and a wife, your left hand should push them away,
your right hand should draw them close (Sota).

Do not throw a stone in a well from which you drank water
(Baba Kama).

Resh Lakish said, "Teaching children is more important than
building the Temple."

CHAPTER TEN

SOCIAL LIFE AND ETHICS

For generations, Jewish life has been guided by religious customs, ethics and social life. These ethics and customs, based upon the teachings of the Torah and the Talmud, helped the Jews to remain one entity in the midst of a world full of superstition, bigotry, violence and enmity. In this chapter, the reader will find some of the customs and ethical ideas, in brief and simple form, by which the Jews have lived for generations, and also the reasons behind them.

SPECIFIC LAWS GOVERNING CRIME AND PUNISHMENT

The sages taught that a man commits a crime, not because he is a criminal at heart, but because of circumstances for which he is not responsible. They said that a Baal Teshubah (a repentant man) is greater than the most pious man, since it is easy for a pious man to be good, but for one of weaker flesh this may prove difficult. The sages decreed that a man who had committed a crime should be warned before he is punished, for either he was ignorant of the law or had acted unconsciously.

When brought into court a criminal had to be confronted by two witnesses of the crime. The witnesses were examined in separate chambers to make sure the testimony of one corroborated the testimony of the other. The court consisted of seventy-one judges including the high priest acting as the presiding judge. It was called the Great Sanhedrin. There were also district Sanhedrin (courts) consisting of twenty-three members. Conviction could be obtained by a majority of two judges. A majority of only one was necessary to free a suspect. The Sanhedrin was always reluctant to pass a death sentence, as it feared to be known as a Beth Din Katlanit (a killing court).

Human life was so sacred to the Jew that even a legal killing was repugnant. On the slightest pretext, a condemned man could receive reprieve after reprieve.

Preceding the Sanhedrin, Ezra the Scribe created the Great Assembly (444 B.C.E.) to assist him in enforcing and in creating laws. Since the Council was made up of the most learned and respected men in the country, it enjoyed tremendous prestige. The first debates recorded in the Talmud took place in the Great Council or Assembly. It enacted among many laws the chanting of the eighteen prayers or the Shmone Esrei.

Later, during the Hasmonean dynasty, the Great Council became the great Sanhedrin. The Sanhedrin was not only a legislative body, but also an academy of learning. When Judea was made a province of Rome by Pompey, the San-hedrin lost its political and law enforcement powers.

It is interesting to note that just as the Sanhedrin consisted of seventy members, with the high priest as the presiding judge making seventy-one, so the College of Cardinals of the Catholic Church consists of seventy members with the Pope making seventy-one.

PRAYER

The Jews have, since the days of the prophet Samuel, adopted the approach of silent prayer and meditation, in honor of

Samuel's mother, Hannah, who was the first to pray silently.

Praying to one God began in the days of Abraham. In early periods praying was impromptu. Sacrifice took the place of prayer in many cases, as a ritual to approach God.

When the Temples were destroyed, prayers replaced sacrifices completely. The sages had to accomplish three things:

1. To keep the Jewish people united.
2. To strengthen their religion and traditions.
3. To make their future secure as a nation among other (not always friendly) nations.

To accomplish all these things they combined a set of prayers from the Torah, Talmud and Holy writings and included poems and prayers written by sages. It was then decreed that these prayers be chanted by all Jews at set times. Thus, on Sabbath and the Festivals, the Jews of distant countries chanted the same prayers at the same time. This uniformity of prayer created a spiritual unity which transcended physical separation, brought strength to the few in the knowledge of their oneness with many. All these prayers, with small variations, were combined into one book, the Siddur, used by the Jews throughout the centuries.

During morning praying, every orthodox Jew over thirteen years of age, wears a Talith and Tefilin. The Talith is the shawl with fringes (Tzitzith), which when counted, together with their knots, number 613, which is the number of all the commandments given to man by God, and also, supposedly, represents the number of organs and veins of the human body. It is worn every morning, while praying, as a symbol of willingness to serve God with all one's might. There is also a Talith Katon (a small Talith) worn by Jews. When a Jew dies, he is wrapped in his Talith for burial. The Talith is white with blue stripes; the white symbolizes peace on earth, and the heavenly blue denotes "God's sanction." If God's commandments will be observed, there will be peace on earth. Some Talethim have black stripes as a symbol of the destruction of the Temples.

The Tefilin, or Phylacteries, are put on for morning prayers except on Holidays. It is incumbent upon every Jew, thirteen years old and over, to do so. The Phylacteries consist of two leather boxes to which straps are attached. The leather must come from a Kosher animal. One of these boxes is wound about the left arm near the region of the heart, the other is fastened to the forehead. Inside the box which is placed on the arm first, there is one parchment scroll. Inside the box which is placed on the head, there are four scrolls. The inscriptions on those scrolls carry the story of the Exodus from Egypt, which teaches that by serving God, the Jews will become free. The inscriptions also carry the Shema (portion from the Torah) which tells the Jews to love God with all their heart, soul and might. The Phylacteries are placed on the head and left arm, near the heart, to symbolize that God can be served by combining mind and heart. It implies too that the Jews should combine their service to God with good deeds toward their fellow men (Mind, Heart, Hand). While praying, it is customary to wear a Yarmolke (skull cap) to denote that God is always above. Pious Jews wear a Yarmolke constantly.

MINYAN (*A basic institution which kept democracy strong among Jews*)

It was incumbent upon every Jew to visit the Holy Temple at Jerusalem at least three times a year: during the holidays of Passover, Shavuoth and Sukkoth (The Shalosh Regalim). At the base of this requirement lay a broad purpose. All the Jews were brought together to stress the unity of the people. Groups from different regions met and derived a cosmopolitan outlook on life. Further, this afforded the Priests and Levites an opportunity for constant instruction.

After the destruction of the Temples (586 B.C.E. and 70 C.E.), when the Jews were dispersed throughout the world, the Rabbis decreed that all Jews should gather in their synagogues three times a day.

The Minyan or quorum, for that purpose, consisted of ten males, thirteen years old or over. These gatherings preserved the unity of the Jews. They also preserved democracy among them. Nine men, however highly placed, did not constitute a Minyan; while any ten men, regardless of their station of life, did. Everyone had equal rights in a Minyan. The thrice daily meetings were not only for prayer but also for study and discussion of religious, civil and communal matters. The Jews, during their darkest days, could gather in their synagogues and feel a sense of unity and strength, and a restoration of their hopes and spirit. The Synagogue is therefore called, not only the house of worship, but also the house of study and the house of assembly.

THE SYNAGOGUE

The Synagogues and Temples took the place of the destroyed ancient Temples. In ancient days, the religious needs of the Temples were administered by the Kohanim and by the Levites. The religious needs of the present day Synagogues and Temples are administered by the Rabbi of the Congregation, the Chazan and the Shamash.

THE RABBI is a person well versed in Jewish religious and civil laws, who has been ordained (received Semicha) as a Rabbi, to perform all religious functions necessary in a Jewish community. Many people make the mistake of calling "Rabbi" any man associated with Jewish religious life, whether he is a teacher, Shamash or Chazan. This is incorrect. The first sages, like Hillel, Shemaiah, and Shammai, were called by their first names, without any title. The Tanaim after them— creators of the Mishna—had the title of Rabbi, like Rabbi Akiba. The Amoraim who followed (creators of the Gemara) had the title "Rav." Then followed the title of "Rabban," like Rabban Gamaliel, meaning head of the academy. Then came "Gaon" meaning genius (Saadia Gaon). After that they reverted to the title "Rabbi," which has become customary and is still used. The word "Rabbi" comes from the word "Rav," which means "much" and signifies a man of much learning.

THE CHAZAN (Cantor) is the person who chants the prayer before the congregation. He is called Sh'liach Tzibur, representative of the congregation, because he represents the people before God in their prayers. He must be a pious man.

THE SHAMASH (Server) is the sexton, who helps in the affairs of the Synagogue. He is the "all-around" man in the congregation. In many instances he is also the Ba'al Koreh, the reader of the Torah.

On the Sabbath and other Holidays, it is the custom to read portions from the Torah and Prophets, as decreed by Ezra and the Great Assembly in 444 B.C.E. A number of men are called to chant the blessings over the Torah. On the Sabbath, seven men are called up; on Yom Kippur, six; on Rosh Hashanah, Sukkoth, Passover and Shavuoth five men are called up; on Rosh Chodesh and Chol Hamoed—four, on Monday, Thursday, Saturday afternoon, Chanukah and Purim only three men are called up.

The men are called up to the Bimah or pulpit, in front of the Aron Kodesh (the Holy Ark), in which the scrolls of the Torah are kept, and which symbolizes the Holy Ark of the Temple, in which the two Tablets with the Ten Commandments were kept. The Aron Kodesh is draped with a Parochet (a drape), and a Ner Tamid (perpetual light) is hanging in front of the Aron Kodesh. It symbolizes perpetual eternity of the Torah, which is inside the Ark.

The ancient Temple was supported financially and otherwise through national taxes and sacrifices. Modern Synagogues and Temples are supported by the community in which they are located. The financial affairs are usually administered by a board of trustees. Most of the Synagogues and Temples have religious schools as part of their religious life. The present day Temple and Synagogue is called Beth Tefilah, Beth Knesseth, and Beth Midrash (House of Prayer, House of Assembly, and House of Study).

Dietary Laws

Jewish religious tradition requires the eating of food which is Kosher, meaning ritually clean, in accordance with definite rules, regulations and rituals. (Treifa means not Kosher.)

Meat is considered Kosher if it meets the following requirements and receives the following treatment: Only animals that have split hooves, and chew their cud may be selected, and the general health of the animal must be good. Then the animal is slaughtered by a Shochet (ritual slaughterer) according to certain techniques prescribed by Jewish law. The animal must be free of broken bones, cancerous growth, dangerous disfigurations and abnormal conditions of a vital organ. If there is any doubt, a Rabbi should be consulted. This consultation is called asking a Sheilah (a question).

Next, the meat is made ready for cooking. It must be soaked for half an hour in water and salted for an hour on a sloping board in order to drain away the blood. (It is forbidden for Jews to consume blood.) It is then rinsed three times. Liver, because of its abundance of blood, must be broiled over a direct fire.

Fish and fowl must meet different requirements from animals in order to be considered Kosher. Only fish which have scales and fins may be eaten; therefore, shell-fish are forbidden. As to fowl, only those may be eaten which have a crop, an extra joint in their legs, have not been attacked by a bird or animal, are not birds of prey and are not sick.

The dietary laws also forbid the mixing of meat with dairy foods and dishes. A dairy meal may follow a meat meal only after an interval of six hours. Meat dishes may be consumed one-half hour following a dairy dish.

These dietary laws, together with their laws governing cleanliness, have kept the Jews healthy throughout their long history.

PERSECUTION FOR OBSERVING LAWS OF CLEANLINESS

During the Middle Ages, the Bubonic Plague (1348) swept Europe, and a quarter of the population died. The Jews suffered little, due to the observance of their religious laws of cleanliness. They washed their hands before eating, as prescribed by law, bathed in their Mikvas (pools), observed dietary laws, kept their food covered, abstained from eating meat of sick animals and fowl, and rested after eating. Their burial observances in which the body is kept comparatively isolated and clean, also minimized contagion. The stricken population however, could not understand why the Jews were not also affected by the plague, and accused them of witchcraft. Thousands of Jews were killed on these false charges.

Origin of False Accusation that Jews Use Blood of Christians

Though Jews are forbidden to taste any blood whatsoever, and therefore salt their meat before cooking it, an accusation that Jews drank the blood of Christians was raised in Europe against them. It started in Norwich, England, during the inauguration of Richard the Lionhearted (1144). A rumor circulated that Jews had killed a Christian in order to use his blood for ritual purposes, and a mob set out to kill them. It is to King Richard's credit that he sent troops to disperse the mob.

Later, this accusation spread like wild-fire throughout Europe. Time and again, Jews were charged with using Christian blood instead of wine for Passover. The charge was used repeatedly by unscrupulous rulers to divert the people from their oppressors. In Russia, particularly, where the people were under the oppression of the Czars, this tactic of divide and conquer was applied in anti-semitic drum-beating. During the reign of the last Czar, blood-drinking charges were brought against a Russian Jew, Mendel Beilis. The horrified reaction of the civilized world finally compelled the court to free him.

MARRIAGE

According to Jewish tradition, marriage is a custom sanctified by God. When the groom places the ring on the bride's finger, he says, "You are hereby sanctified unto me by this ring according to the law of Moses and Israel."

In the Jewish religion, the marriage ring has to be smooth and without any stones or carvings, as a symbol of a smooth and rounded, happy wedded life. It does not stand for slavery, as some people think. It is simply a token of good will, pledging that the written contract will be fulfilled. In ancient days, either a coin or some other token was used in place of a ring. During the marriage ceremony the bride does not promise to obey her husband like a slave; both bride and groom promise to honor and cherish each other.

The Kethuba is a marriage agreement between bride and groom. In it, they vow to cherish, honor and care for each other. The agreement or proclamation is signed by non-relatives. It is read during the marriage ceremony by the Rabbi. The Kethuba includes a traditional point, a promise to the wife of 200 Zuzim for her protection in case of divorce.

The Chuppah is the canopy held aloft over the heads of the bride and groom during the marriage ceremony. It is the symbol of their future home.

At the conclusion of the ceremony, the groom breaks a glass to remind them of the destruction of the Temple. Thus, at every celebration, Jews are urged to remember their historical background in the land of Israel.

The marriage ceremony is a happy occasion. It is not performed during fast days, or when counting the Omer (see Holidays), except for the day of Lag B'Omer. Neither is the ceremony allowed on Holidays, since they themselves are happy occasions, and Jews are urged not to confuse one happiness with another. (Ein M'arvin Simcha B'simcha: You do not mix one happiness with another.)

CIRCUMCISION

The Hebrew word for circumcision is Brith Milah, meaning Covenant. God commanded Abraham to circumcise all males of his household as a sign of a covenant between God and Abraham and his descendants.

Circumcision has nothing to do with human sacrifice, as some people think. While offering of a human life was commonplace in the religions of ancient man, Jews have always opposed it. So repugnant was the practice to Abraham the Hebrew, that it took the command of the Almighty Himself to induce him to deliver his son Isaac as a sacrifice. Satisfied with Abraham's devotion, God substituted a ram, indicating His displeasure with human sacrifices.

A man trained and religiously qualified for the service, performs the circumcision. He is called the Mohel.

The man who holds the child during the ceremony is called the Sandek. To be a Sandek is considered an honor.

DIVORCE

Divorce in Hebrew is called Get. According to Jewish Law, a divorce is easily obtained, provided both parties agree. The law urges, however, that the Rabbi allow an interval to elapse before granting a divorce. During this period he makes every effort to reconcile the couple. In many cases wise counselling of a sympathetic third party can preserve the home. If, however, the Rabbi becomes convinced that there can be no agreement, he grants a divorce.

The divorce is written out and presented to the wife in the presence of two witnesses whose signatures it carries. She must then wait ninety days before she is allowed to marry. She must also bear in mind that, if she marries a second time, she can never remarry her first husband.

The Jewish divorce laws are advanced even for modern times. In the United States today, there are some authorities who would substitute them for our State laws which are archaic in comparison.

MOURNING

When a person dies, it is incumbent upon the nearest relative to observe the law of Keriah ceremony (making a small rip in one's garments) as a sign of mourning. For parents, the tear is made on the left side of one's garment; for other relatives, on the right side. Part of the burial service consists of the "Hesped" or eulogy of the departed one. This custom dates from Abraham when he eulogized Sarah, at her death.

SHIVAH, which in Hebrew means seven, is observed by the mourner for seven days. During this period the bereaved is not permitted to work. He remains at home, sitting on a low bench. At the mourner's first meal, eggs are served, symbolizing the cycle of life and death. Life, like an egg, is round. . . . Generations go, and generations come and replace them.

If a person dies and is buried a few hours before sundown on the eve of Passover, Shavuoth, Sukkoth, Rosh Hashanah or Yom Kippur, the mourner does not have to sit shivah after the holiday. The Sabbath is counted as one of the seven days, although no public mourning is allowed.

174

KADDISH The Kaddish or memorial prayer, is recited daily, from the day of burial for eleven months. The Kaddish prayer is a prayer of glorification of God. The word Kaddish comes from the Hebrew, "Kadosh," which means "holy." There is no mention of death in the Kaddish. In ancient days, Kaddish was said after the study of the Torah and Talmud. It continues to be done this way today, but it became a duty in later years to say it in memory of departed ones. This shows that one accepts the judgment of God, the Supreme Judge, and glorifies his name, as God has given and God has taken.

YORTZEIT means in Yiddish the anniversary of death. Every year, on the day of its occurrence, a special prayer is chanted, the (K)Eil Mole Rachamim (God is full of compassion). The mourner lights a candle (the light of a candle symbolizes peace to the soul); and gives alms. Charity may take many forms, donations of money, donations of work or good deeds.

YZKOR means to remember. Four times a year, on Yom Kippur, on Shemini Atzeret, on the last day of Passover, and on the second day of Shavuoth, one says extra prayers for his departed ones, and promises to give Tz'dakah (charity).

Pidyon Haben

The source of this tradition is the Torah, where the story is told of how the Angel spared the Jewish first born in Egypt, when he slew the first born Egyptians. Hence it is considered that every first born child, if a boy, belongs to God. The Kohen (priest), as the representative of God, has to release the boy when he becomes thirty days old. At a special ceremony, the father gives to the Kohen five dollars or coin

175

equivalent to the five shekalim as prescribed in the Torah, and the Kohen releases the boy. The son of a Kohen, or of a daughter of a Levite, is exempted from this ceremony.

BAR MITZVAH

Bar Mitzvah implies a boy's maturity, when he can be enrolled as a member of the Jewish community and can assume the responsibiity of observing the commandments of the Torah. When a Jewish boy becomes thirteen years of age, his induction into the Jewish community is celebrated with appropriate ceremonies.

He is called up to the reading of the Torah. There he recites two blessings, thanking God for giving the Jews the Torah. He chants a portion from the Prophets called the Haphtorah. Each Saturday a different Haphtorah is chanted and different Sedrot or portions from the Torah are read. This custom was initiated by Ezra the Scribe, after the return of the Jews from Babylon.

One month before his Bar Mitzvah ceremony (or date of birth), the candidate has to don Tefilin every morning, except on Holidays, to signify his acceptance of his responsibilities as a Jewish man.

THE JEWISH CALENDAR

The word *month* in Hebrew is "Yerach," from the Hebrew "Yareach," meaning moon. It denotes that the Jewish calendar is lunar. The calendar consists of 12 months. In a leap year, it consists of 13 months, to even out the difference between the lunar and solar calendars, which contain 354 and 365 days respectively. Some months contain 29 days, some 30.

The Jewish calendar as used today was finally arranged by Hillel the second in 360 C.E. The names of the months are as follows:

Tishri, Chesvan, Kislev, Tebeth, Shevat, Adar Alef, Adar Beth, Nisan, Iyar, Sivan, Tamuz, Ab, Elul.

Although the Mohammedan calendar is also a lunar one, it does not compensate with an extra month in a leap year. Consequently, few Mohammedan festivals fall in the seasons they are designed to celebrate.

CHAPTER ELEVEN

JEWISH HOLIDAYS AND FAST DAYS

In this chapter, the definition of Jewish holidays and the customs accompanying them, will be detailed. The holidays follow in order of their observance during the year. As Rosh Hashanah, the Jewish New Year, is the first holiday observed, it appears first in the first month of the year, namely, Tishri. The rest of the holidays follow in order.

HOLIDAY

A holiday is a day made sacred by religious decree, or a day of observance commemorating a very special event. It is a day on which man rests from his labors. He prays, sings songs, holds discussions and studies. This routine is traditional and, from a religious stand-point, mandatory.

THREE SYNONYMS IN HEBREW FOR THE WORD HOLIDAY

Atzereth: gathering.
Moed: a time that has been specially set aside.
Chag: a celebration.

Together these three words describe the full import of the term "holiday": a gathering at a specially designated time for a celebration.

In all holidays, the community of man is stressed; the joining of the spiritual and temporal; the worship of God, and the forging of stronger bonds among free men. In song and discussions and study, the holiday fortifies man and sends him forth refreshed to meet the coming days.

YOM TOV means a good day. Every holiday is called a Yom Tov.

THE SABBATH

Literally Sabbath means to rest. It is a day different from the other six days of the week. Spiritually, it means a period spent in religious thought and contemplation. The exhortation expressed in the Torah, to keep the seventh day as a day of rest, cultural development and freedom, is of special significance. If a man is required to have at least one day free each week, then he will remain free at all times. Slaves have no day to call their own. The Sabbath also proclaims God as the Creator of the Universe. He rested on the seventh day; man, who is the highest of His creations, follows His example.

TIME OF OBSERVANCE   The Sabbath is observed from sundown to sundown on every seventh day. We begin every Jewish holiday at sundown because the Torah tells us that God, when He created the world, considered the evening as the beginning of the next day, as it is written: "And there was evening, and there was morning."

LIGHTING OF SABBATH CANDLES   Two candles or more, depending upon the community custom, are lit every Friday evening as a symbol of peace, freedom and the light which radiates from the human soul. The mother, considered by the sages as the guiding influence of the Jewish family, has the privilege of lighting the candles. She does so also, because

Eve, the first mother, prevented eternal life by disobeying God's command not to eat from the tree of knowledge. The present-day mother, by lighting the candles, prays for a long life of happiness and peace for her family.

While making the blessing, the mother or wife covers her eyes. The reason for it is: A blessing should be made before an action. The light of a candle ushers in the Sabbath. Since it is not permitted to light the candles on the Sabbath itself, she avoids this dilemma by covering her eyes so as not to see the light, makes the blessing, and then looks at the light. Thus the Sabbath is ushered in and the candles are lit.

KIDDUSH   Kiddush is a blessing over wine. It is said on the Sabbath and on holidays. The male head of the household chants the Kiddush in memory of the bondage in Egypt, and pledges that never again will the Jews tolerate slavery. Kiddush ushers in the sacred feeling of Sabbath and other holidays.

SERVICES FOR SABBATH

KABOLATH SHABBATH (welcoming of the Sabbath) service chanted on Friday before sundown.

MA'ARIV (evening prayers) service follows.

THE SHACHARITH (morning prayers)   On Saturday morning, the Shacharith is chanted, followed by the reading of a specific weekly portion of the Torah. The first person called is a Kohen, a descendant of Aaron, the brother of Moses and first high priest. After the Kohen, a Levi (a descendant of the tribe of Levi) is called. The Kohen and the Levi are especially honored because they were the spiritual leaders and teachers of the Jews in Egypt and in the Promised Land.

The reading culminates with the reading of a portion from the Prophets (called the Haphtorah).

The morning service is terminated with the chanting of the *Mussaf* (from the Hebrew *Nosaf,* meaning added), additional morning prayers.

In the afternoon, the *Mincha* (afternoon service) is chanted.

BEST KNOWN SABBATH PRAYERS AND CHANTS

1. L'CHA DODI (Go forth my beloved): recited on Friday evening. A poem written by Solomon the Levite (Alkabetz) in the 16th Century. The first letters of the lines in each stanza spell out the author's name. In it Jews extol the Sabbath created by God, and express the belief that the Messiah, descended from David, will appear in the Holy City of Jerusalem and defeat Israel's enemies.

2. V'SHAMRU (the Jews shall observe the Sabbath): Excerpt from the Torah commanding the Jews to observe the Sabbath.

3. VAYECHULU (and thus were finished): Excerpt from the Torah describing how God rested on the seventh day. V'shamru and Vayechulu are recited every Friday evening.

4. SHALOM ALEICHEM (peace be with you): When coming home from the synagogue on Friday night the Jew chants this famous song welcoming the angels of peace into his home.

5. (K)EIL ADON (God is the Lord): chanted on Sabbath morning. In this prayer is described the control God exercises over planets, stars, sun, moon, earth and all creatures.

6. YISMACH MOSHE (Moses shall rejoice): in which happiness over the Torah is expressed.
7. BRICH SHME (Blessed be His name): from the Zohar —written in Aramaic, in which the Jew prays to the Lord that he may never have to depend upon man but upon God alone. He says this prayer before the reading of the Torah and before an open Aron Kodesh (Holy Ark).
8. TIKANTAH SHABBATH (Thou hast created the Sabbath): in which the Jew prays for an opportunity to celebrate Sabbath in Jerusalem. It is chanted in the Mussaf service.
9. YISMECHU (They shall rejoice): the Sabbath observers shall rejoice over the beauty of the Sabbath.
10. EIN K'ELO(K)ENU (None is like our Lord): this familiar song is popular among young and old.

SHALOSH S'UDOTH

Though Shalosh S'udoth means "three meals," it refers to the third and last meal eaten after Mincha service on the Sabbath. The three meals of Sabbath served a very important purpose and still do. Socially it strengthens family ties, as the family gathers around the Sabbath table to dine together and join in songs and discussions.

SPECIAL DISHES AND FOODS OF SABBATH

TWO CHALOTH (twist breads) are used on Friday evenings, Saturdays and Holidays, as a symbol of the Manna which fed the Jews in the desert. The Jews gathered a measure each day and a double measure on Friday, so that they might rest on the Sabbath. The Chaloth therefore, symbolize rest.

The cloth with which the Chaloth are covered symbolizes

183

the dew, which covered the Manna in the desert to keep it from spoiling.

GEFILTE FISH (stuffed fish) symbolizes the huge, mythical fish called the Leviathan, which feeds forever all the Sabbath-observing pious souls in Paradise. Gefilte fish is a traditional dish eaten on the Sabbath and other holidays.

KUGEL A round pudding prepared for the Sabbath, as is the Cholent. It comes from the Hebrew, K'Agol, like a circle. It symbolizes a round good week.

CHOLENT Cholent originated among the Jews of France. It may be any or several of a number of characteristic dishes (candied potatoes and prunes, barley and lima beans, peas and barley, meat and potatoes, etc.) cooked over-night and eaten the next day on the Sabbath. The word comes from the French "Chaleur," meaning warmth, and from the Hebrew "Shelan," meaning that which stayed overnight.

HAVDALAH (*separation*)

At the ceremony of Havdalah, a blessing is made over wine on Saturday night, to indicate the division between the Sabbath and midweek, between light and darkness. The blessings are made by the light of a long candle, to symbolize the first man, Adam, who discovered the existence of fire. A blessing is also chanted over spices, to denote a fragrant week.

After the Havdalah, it is customary to greet each other with the words "A Gutte Voch," meaning, "Let there be a good week."

M'LAVE MALKA (Farewell to the Queen): The Sabbath is considered a queen who has come to stay for one day. In honor of her visit the Jew puts on his best clothes and serves his best food. When she is ready to depart, he gives her a suitable farewell. He sings Zemiroth (songs), and discusses Torah questions while eating.

SELICHOTH

Special prayers of forgiveness (from the Hebrew "Selicha" meaning forgiveness) are recited every midnight, approximately during the week before Rosh Hashanah. This is done to show our sincere belief in God which prevails day and night.

ROSH HASHANAH (*Jewish New Year*)

Rosh Hashanah means the beginning of the year. It is celebrated on the first and second days of the month of Tishri (September), because tradition tells us that the world was then created. Rosh Hashanah is observed for two days even in Israel, where some holidays are celebrated for one day only. Rosh Hashanah is also known as the Day of Remembrance and the Day of Judgment. It is a day of man's judgment by God, when his good and bad deeds are reviewed. This holiday, whose two days are considered as one long day (Yoma Arichta), is also known as Yom Teruah, the day of the blowing of the Shofar (ram's horn). The blowing of the Shofar symbolizes three different expressions of the human spirit and denotes faith in God.

1. Tekiah (long sound) denotes triumph of God.
2. Shevarim (broken sounds) denotes weeping.
3. Teruah (tremolo) denotes alarm.

The Shofar goes back to the time when Abraham was ready to sacrifice his only son Isaac at God's behest. At the last moment, the Almighty permitted Abraham to substitute a ram. The Jewish people seek to recall, by blowing the horn, the complete faith of the first Hebrew, Abraham. The story of the sacrifice (called the Akeida) is read in the Torah on the second day of Rosh Hashanah.

After services, Jews greet each other with "L'shanah Tovah Tikatevu," which means, "May you be inscribed in the book of life for the next year."

To perform Tashlich (throwing away), Jews go to a river or other body of running water. There they symbolically throw off their sins to be carried away by the water.

They eat a round Challah, as a symbol of a round, smooth, happy New Year. They taste honey to symbolize a sweet New Year, and pray that the Lord shall give them a sweet New Year. They eat a new fruit, also dates, pomegranates, apples, etc.

In the blessing of She'Hecheyanu, Jews thank God for keeping them alive until now.

Jews also eat Tzimes, a dish made of carrots. The Yiddish word for carrots is "meyrin" which also means to increase or to multiply. They therefore eat Tzimes on Rosh Hashanah as a symbol of God multiplying their advantages.

TEN DAYS OF PENITENCE

The ten days beginning with the first day of Rosh Hashanah and ending with Yom Kippur are called the Ten Days of Penitence. During these days, the Jews make a greater effort to show that they regret their sins.

FAST OF GEDALIAH (586 B.C.E.)

After the destruction of the first Temple, the king of Babylon, Nebuchadnezzar, appointed a Jewish governor over Judea.

This Governor Gedaliah and his appointment portended a flourishing of Jewish community life in Israel. Unfortunately, a group of Jewish soldiers, incited by Egypt, murdered Gedaliah. With his death, the chance for a Jewish culture in Israel was lost for a long time. The whole course of Jewish history may well have been altered had Gedaliah lived. The fast of Gedaliah is observed on the day after Rosh Hashanah.

YOM KIPPUR

Yom Kippur (the Day of Atonement) falls on the tenth day of the Jewish month of Tishri (September-October). It is the most solemn day in the Jewish calendar. Because penitence, prayer and charity can alter evil, the Day of Atonement is spent in fasting, praying and committing oneself to a worthy cause.

KOL NIDRE (all vows) is recited before sundown on the eve of Yom Kippur. It is a declaration that all vows and promises made by man to God and to himself during the past year which have been overlooked, shall be null and void. Vows and promises made by man to his fellow man, however, are not voided by the declaration of Kol Nidre, since broken promises are considered a heavy sin according to law.

The well-known melody of Kol Nidre is believed to have originated among the Marranos in Spain. The Marranos were Jews forcibly converted to Christianity who secretly observed their religion, often at great peril. Since they were the victims of force, they considered their promises to observe Christianity as meaningless.

EXCERPT FROM THE PROPHETS READ ON YOM KIPPUR We read about the Prophet Jonah, sent by God to preach in

Nineveh, the wicked Assyrian city. He tried to escape his responsibility and ran away. While at sea he was thrown overboard by his fellow travelers. A whale swallowed him and brought him back. Jonah finally realized that there is no escape from God. This lesson is recalled to the Jews on the Day of Atonement and fasting.

NE'ILAH (closing) is the final service of Yom Kippur, said just before sundown when the gates of heaven close. It is the Jewish belief that the gates of heaven are open especially during the ten days of Penitence, to receive the prayers of all people.

SUKKOTH (*huts*)

Sukkoth is considered the Jewish Thanksgiving day and is celebrated from the 15th to the 22nd day of Tishri (October). It includes two other holiday celebrations called Hoshanah Rabbah and Shemini Atzereth.

Sukkoth is the holiday of huts. When the Jews lived in the desert after their Exodus from Egypt, they gathered and dwelt in huts and tents. After settling in Israel, they again utilized small huts during harvest time, as temporary dwellings. This holiday is therefore called the Holiday of Huts (Chag Hasukkoth) as well as the Holiday of Gathering (Chag He'asif).

The following are used on Sukkoth:

THE ETHROG or citron fruit symbolizes individuals who are both educated and have good deeds to their credit.

THE LULAV or branch of a palm tree represents people with great wealth, but without good deeds to their credit.

188

THE HADAS or myrtle branch symbolizes people who are educated, but do not use their knowledge for the welfare of their fellowmen.

THE ARAVAH or willow branch symbolizes people without education, without money and without good deeds.

These are all used simultaneously. The blessing chanted over them denotes unity of all people. In preparation for the proper blessings, the Ethrog must be held in the left hand, while the Lulav, together with three myrtle branches and two willow branches, is held in the right hand.

HOSHANAH RABBAH

Meals are eaten in huts for seven days to commemorate the forefathers' dwelling in huts. On the seventh day of Sukkoth, called Hoshanah Rabbah, willow branches called Hoshanoth, are used in conjunction with prayers. They represent:

1. *The renewal of life:* Old leaves fall off, new ones grow in the Spring. Old generations pass, new ones take their place.

2. *The Babylonian captivity:* When the Jews were exiled to Babylon, after the destruction of the first Temple (586 B.C.E.), they were commanded by their captors to entertain them by playing happy songs. The Jews hung their instruments on willow branches and refused to play while their Temple was being destroyed. This is one of the reasons no musical instruments are played in Orthodox Synagogues. It is believed that on Hoshanah Rabbah, God seals his final decision as to the fate of each person for the forthcoming year. On that night, according to legend, the heavens split open

189

for one brief moment and anyone who makes a wish at that particular time will have his wish fulfilled.

SHEMINI ATZERETH (*eighth day of the holiday*)

The eighth day of Sukkoth is called Shemini Atzereth. On that day, Jews pray for rain in Israel. Israel is an agricultural country with a scarcity of water. By praying for rain for Israel, Jews of other countries show their solidarity with the Jews of Israel. On Shemini Atzereth, they say special Memorial Prayers for their dear departed, as they do on Yom Kippur, on the last day of Passover and on Shavuoth.

SIMCHAT TORAH (*rejoicing over the Torah*)

The day after Sukkoth or Shemini Atzereth is called Simchat Torah. The Jews parade in a circle inside the synagogue seven or more rounds (called in Hebrew "Hakafoth"), a different worshiper holding the scrolls of the Torah on each round. Children carry flags with suitable inscriptions. All sing and dance, rejoicing in their great inheritance, the Torah. Before the Hakafoth, special verses called the Ata Haretah, are read by assigned people, who are considered honored by being so selected. People have been known to contribute large sums of money to charity for this privilege.

Jews rejoice on Simchat Torah because the reading of the last chapters of the Torah is finished and the reading of the first book is begun. This signifies that the Torah has no beginning and no end. On Simchat Torah, small children, who are not yet Bar-Mitzvah and thus not entitled to be called up to the Torah, on this day of the year only, with a Talis (prayer shawl) over their heads, are recognized as future congregants, and called up to recite the blessings over the Torah in unison.

CHANUKAH (*Dedication*)

Chanukah is called the holiday of Dedication and also the holiday of lights. It is celebrated on the 25th day of Kislev (December) for eight days.

When the Jews were under the domination of the Syrian Greeks (160 B. C. E.), King Antioches tried to force the Jews to abandon their religion, traditions and customs. The Jews refused and rebelled. The revolt was led by the eighty-year-old Kohen, Matathias, the Hasmonean, and his five brave sons. Of the latter, the best known was Judah the Maccabee (the hammer), who became the leader after his father's death. He defeated the Greeks and once again, the Jews were free in their own land. Judah dedicated the Temple and lit the Menorah (lamp). That is why Jews call it the Holiday of Chanukah or Dedication, and also the "Holiday of Lights." Judah was called the Maccabee because on his flag were the letters, M.K.B.YE, an abbreviation of the words, "Mi Kamocha Baelim Adoshem," "Who is like thee, O Lord, among gods?"

THE TWO MIRACLES OF CHANUKAH

1. *The miracle of the jar of oil* After the heathens had been defeated and driven out, the first wish of the Jewish people was to relight the Lamp or Menorah at the altar of the Temple. They found only a small jar of oil that had not been defiled, and on which there was the seal of the Kohen Gadol (high priest) to attest to its purity. There was just enough oil to last for one day; yet, miraculously, it lasted for eight days. In memory of this miracle, Jews light candles for eight days, and the holiday of Chanukah is therefore also called the Holiday of Lights.

2. *The victory of the Jews over the Greeks,* who greatly outnumbered them, is considered the second miracle.

THE OTHER MEANING OF THE WORD CHANUKAH

The word Chanukah is composed of the two words Chanu and Kah. Chanu means, they rested. The letter K represents the number twenty, and the letter H represents five. The meaning of Chanukah is therefore, "The Jews rested on the twenty fifth of Kislev."

SPECIAL PRACTICES FOLLOWED ON CHANUKAH

Candles are lit for eight nights as a symbol of the miracle of the jar of oil found in the Temple, which burned for eight days. One candle is lit on the eve of the first day, two on the second, and so on, up to the eve of the eighth day, when all eight candles are lit. In addition to the required eight candles, there is also an extra candle each night, which is called the Shamash (server), and is used to kindle the other candles. The first candle is put into the Menorah from the person's right side and an additional candle is added to its left each additional night, and lit from left to right.

Plays are often presented about Eliezer and Hannah on this holiday.

Eliezer was a Kohen slain by the Greeks because he refused to eat the meat of a swine.

Hannah was the Jewish mother of seven children who were given the opportunity to save their lives if they would bow to the idol of the king. They all refused and were encouraged by their mother to do so. All the seven boys were slain and Hannah committed suicide. By presenting plays about these heroes and heroines, Jews instill in their children a love for their traditions and pride in their ancestors.

Another form of entertainment, especially for children, is the playing of games with dreidlach (tops tapering to a point from a square form). The Chanukah dreidl symbolizes the two miracles. On its sides are inscribed the Hebrew letters, N, G, H, SH, which are abbreviations for the Hebrew words: Nes, Gadol, Hayah, Sham—meaning, a great miracle happened there. This refers to the miracle of the jar of oil and also to the miracle of the Jews defeating the powerful Greek army. Jewish children receive Chanukah Gelt or Chanukah money from relatives and with that money they play and spin the top to remind them of those miracles.

FOOD EATEN ON CHANUKAH

Latkes (pancakes) symbolize the miracle of Chanukah. The oil or other fat in which they are fried, reminds Jews of the jar of holy oil which was sufficient only for one day yet lasted for eight days. Some believe that it also reminds them of the pancakes which Jewish women made for their soldiers. Some were so hard, the Jews used them as ammunition against the Greek soldiers.

Tu Bishevat (Jewish Arbor Day)

It is celebrated on the 15th day of the month of Shevat (January-February). "Tu" in Hebrew means the number fifteen. On that day new trees are planted in Israel, and Jews throughout the world collect and contribute money for the planting of more trees in Israel. It is also called the Rosh Hashanah (New Year) for trees. Tradition tells that on that day God decides which plants shall survive and which shall die during the coming year. This teaches that trees and plants are living organisms and should be well cared for.

A people who for centuries were forced to live in dark, drab ghettoes, where vegetation was almost completely absent, find in Tu Bishevat a particular joy.

PURIM (*Persian for Lots*)

It was Haman who drew lots to determine the day on which to kill all Jews.

Purim is a holiday of victory and celebration, and honors the great queen Esther or Hadassah, one of the wives of Ahasverus, who together with her cousin Mordecai, saved their people from extinction.

The Persian Emperor, Ahasuerus, had as his Prime Minister, a despot known as Haman, who sought the complete subjugation of the Jews. When Mordecai, the Jewish leader and patriot, refused repeatedly to bow down before him, Haman plotted the extermination of all Jews in the Empire. Mordecai brought the news of the plot to Queen Esther. At the risk of her life, she interceded for her people. At a banquet that she had prepared for them alone, the king and Haman heard for the first time that Esther was a Jew and could be included in the mass murder. Enraged, the king turned on Haman and ordered him hanged. The Jews were saved, and Mordecai named as the new minister.

SPECIAL THINGS DONE ON PURIM

1. *The Megilah* (scroll) *of Esther,* or the story of Purim, is read.
2. During the reading of the Megilah, the children make derisive noises on Gragers (rattles) whenever the name of Haman is mentioned.
3. A special *Purim Seudah* (Purim feast) is conducted

during Purim Day. It is one of the merriest of Jewish traditional customs.

4. Alms are given to the poor (*Matanot La'evyonim*) and gifts are exchanged by relatives and friends (*Shalach Manot*).

5. A fast day (Fast of Esther) is held on the 13th day of Adar (February-March), the day that Haman was to carry out his plan of extermination.

6. Purim is celebrated on the 14th day of Adar, when the Jews defeated Haman and his co-plotters. During leap years, Purim is celebrated on the 14th of Adar Beth. The day after Purim, called Shushan Purim, is also celebrated, following the practice of the Jews who lived in the Persian capital Shushan (Susa).

7. Poppy-seed pastries called *Hamantashen* are eaten. *Hamantashen* are three-cornered pastries filled with poppy seeds. They symbolize the three-cornered hat of Haman, as well as the feast of Esther at which three people were present (Esther, Haman, and Ahasuerus). The poppy seed is a symbol of the grains of the earth. God promised the Jews that He would make them as numerous as the grains of the earth and that He would keep them from destruction. Kreplach (dumplings filled with meat), are also eaten on Purim, on Hoshanah Rabbah and on the eve of Yom Kippur.

8. Ad Lo Yodah is a Hebrew term used particularly during Purim. It implies happy and carefree celebrating to the point where one is doubtful of the celebrant's sober condition. Literally it means: Ad: until; Lo: did not; Yodah: know.

According to tradition, the Jews were to drink and make merry on Purim until they would not know the difference between cursing Mordecai and blessing Haman. Today, in Israel, a huge public demonstration, called the "Ad Lo Yodah," is staged in Tel Aviv each Purim, with floats and banners depicting the characters and incidents of the story of Purim.

PESACH (*Passover*)

Passover has various names. It is called:

1. The Holiday of Freedom (*Zeman Herutenu*), because on Passover the Jews' bondage ended in Egypt and they became a free people.
2. The Holiday of Spring (*Chag He'aviv*) because it is celebrated in the Spring, beginning with the 15th day of Nisan (April) and lasts eight days.
3. The Holiday of Matzoth (*Chag Ha'Matzoth*), because only unleavened bread (Matzoth) is eaten.
4. Passover (*Pesach*), because the word "Pesach" means to "pass over." When the Angel of Death slew the first-born Egyptians, he passed over the houses of the Israelites.

Passover is a holiday proclaiming freedom and unity, and identifying Jews with their ancestors who ended their bondage in Egypt. It is a holiday of remembrance of the Jews who kept faith with their religion during the long, hard years of slavery. It is a holiday which exalts the freedom God desires for man.

SPECIAL THINGS DONE ON PASSOVER

MAOT CHITIM (literally, money for wheat), is given before Passover to the less fortunate members of the community. In this way, no Jew shall be prevented by want, from properly celebrating the Holiday of Freedom with the rest of the people.

M'CHIRAT CHOMETZ Since, during Passover, the Jew is not permitted to possess any *Chometz* (any food containing in whole or in part, any of the five species of fermented grain, and/or dishes, containers and other implements associated with such food), he is required to effect a sale with a non-Jew for the duration of Passover. This is done through an agent, usually the Rabbi of the community, and is called *M'chirat Chometz,* or selling of the Chometz.

BEDICAT AND BIUR CHOMETZ The ceremony of searching and burning of the Chometz, is observed. The night before Passover pieces of bread are placed on the window sills. Then, by candle light, the bread is brushed into a container with a feather. Feather, candle, and sweepings are burned the following morning.

MATZOTH (thin cakes of flour containing no salt or yeast) are eaten during the eight days of Passover, instead of bread. This commemorates the flight of the Israelites from Egypt. In their hurried escape they took with them, among other things, unleavened dough as part of their food supply. In the desert the unleavened cakes were baked in the heat of the sun.

MATZOH SHEMURAH (Shemurah means "has been watched

197

over"): Since contact of moisture with the wheat kernel starts the process of fermentation almost immediately, watch is maintained over wheat used for Matzoth, so that it remains in the ritual condition.

THE HAGADAH   On the first two nights of Passover the Hagadah (from the Hebrew "L'hagid," meaning "to tell") is read, recounting the story of Passover.

THE SEDER NIGHTS   The first two nights of Passover (the Hebrew word "Seder" means order). Passover is celebrated according to tradition, and in the order prescribed by the sages. This order of procedure is indicated in the Hagadah. During the feast, everybody rests back in the manner of a free and independent people. It was an ancient, oriental custom for free people to recline while eating.

THE FOUR QUESTIONS   The youngest of the family asks the Fier Kashes (the four questions) requesting an explanation for the ceremonial acts performed on Passover. In reply, the father relates the story of Jewish oppression in Egypt, and their Exodus (1300 B.C.E.). The reasons Matzoth, Maror, etc., are eaten are indicated in the Hagadah.

THE TEN PLAGUES   Part of the recital is the story of the Ten Plagues, with which God afflicted the Egyptians in order to compel them to free the Jews from slavery. When reciting the Ten Plagues, wine is spilled from the cups. According to the sages, Jews should not rejoice when any people, even their enemies, are killed.

THREE MATZOTH are placed on the Seder plate in honor of Kohanim, Levites and Israelites who, while in Egypt, did not forget their language, customs and traditions. The unity of all Jews made the Exodus possible.

There is another reason why three Matzoth are placed on the Seder plate. Ordinarily, on every holiday or Sabbath, two Challoth (loaves of bread) are placed on the table. This, called the Lechem Mishneh (double bread), is necessary for the proper blessing to be made. During Passover, however, Matzoth are used. Since according to tradition, Jews are required on Passover also, to eat from the "Poor Bread" (as Matzoh is called) which cannot be taken from a whole loaf, the middle Matzoh is broken and used. The broken part becomes the Afikomen (dessert) and the remaining piece serves as the "Poor Bread."

MAROR (bitter herbs), usually horse radish, is eaten by Jews as a symbol of the suffering of their ancestors in Egypt. Long leaf lettuce can be used for Maror in place of horse radish. It is, in fact, better than horse radish since lettuce is first sweet and becomes bitter as it grows older. It can thus serve as a reminder of the fact that, when the Jews came to Egypt in the days of Joseph, life was sweet for them, but later became bitter.

CHAROSETH (a mixture of wine, ginger, apples and nuts) is used as a symbol of the mortar the Jews' ancestors made in Egypt while slaves of Pharaoh.

AN EGG AND ROASTED MEAT are used to symbolize the Pascal sacrifice brought to the Temple when the Jews lived in Israel. The egg was chosen to represent the Holiday sacrifice because of its inherent qualities. All other foods are softened by long cooking, but an egg becomes harder. So too, the Jews became stronger, the longer they suffered in Egypt. (Exodus, first chapter.) An egg is also round, symbolizing the cycle of life and death, freedom and oppression. (That is why it is also a custom to serve boiled eggs at the first meal of a mourner.)

SALT WATER is used as a symbol of the tears shed by the Jews' ancestors while in Egypt. The salt water may also symbolize the Red Sea, crossed by the Jews after leaving Egypt.

KARPAS (vegetable) is eaten to symbolize the growth of vegetation in the Spring in the aspect of Passover as the Holiday of Spring. Celery or parsley are used as Karpas.

KNEIDLACH or Matzoh balls are eaten during the Passover meal. They are eaten as a symbol of the rocks which fell upon the enemy when Joshua fought the Canaanites on the eve of Passover. He ordered the sun to stand still so that he might finish the battle before sundown.

DIPPING Karpas is dipped into salt water as a symbol of the miracle of the Red Sea, when it split in two. This took place in the Spring. Maror is dipped into the Charoseth to symbolize the bitterness of life for the Jews in Egypt.

FOUR CUPS OF WINE are consumed, symbolizing the four promises which God made to the Jews in Egypt. They were:

1. "I shall bring you out."
2. "I shall save you."
3. "I shall redeem you."
4. "I shall take you."

A SANDWICH OF MATZOH AND MAROR is eaten on the Seder night. This custom was instituted by the Sage Hillel.

THE CUP OF ELIJAH An extra cup of wine is placed on the

Seder table for the prophet Elijah. The door is opened to admit Elijah, who, it is traditionally held, visits every Jewish home on Passover and blesses the people. Elijah was the most beloved prophet among Jews, and many legends have been told about him. Tradition says that he is the one who will announce the coming of the Messiah.

The fifth cup of wine also symbolizes the fifth promise of God to the Jews in Egypt: "And I shall bring you into the promised land." The Seder night is terminated with the eating of the Afikomen (from the Greek word for "dessert"), consisting of the broken piece of Matzoh which the master of the house concealed at the beginning of the Seder service. It symbolizes the Pascal sacrifice which was partaken of in Temple repasts.

Children play an active part in the Passover celebration because of God's command that the children be told about the Exodus so that they might learn to cherish freedom and be proud of their heritage and traditions.

It has become a practice for the youngest child to recover the Afikomen and demand a ransom from the father for its return. The Seder cannot be ended without it.

CHAD GADYAH   At the end of the Seder service songs are sung, the last of which is *Chad Gadyah (One Only Kid)*. This is a simple song, the moral of which is that God is the Supreme Judge of the Universe.

THE SONG OF SONGS, written by King Solomon, is chanted on the morning of Passover in keeping with the spirit of the holiday, of Spring.

OMER   On the second day of Passover the counting of the Omer is begun. The Omer is a grain measure. The Torah commands Jews to keep count, day by day, of the forty-nine days from Passover to Shavuoth, when the first fruits (first sheaves of grain), the Bikurim, were brought to the Temple.

CHOL HAMOED   The four days between the first two days and last two days of Sukkoth and Passover are called Chol Hamoed (mid-week holiday). These days are considered half-holidays; the first two and the last two are considered full holidays.

LAG BA'OMER

When the Jews were under the domination of Rome, they rose in revolt against their oppressors. The army of rebellion was led by Bar Kochba (132 C.E.), and was inspired by Rabbi Akiba, one of the greatest sages. During the revolt, pupils of Rabbi Akiba died in a plague. On Lag Ba'omer the plague ended. The revolt was finally broken by the Romans, whose overwhelming power no other people dared to defy. Therefore, during the counting of the Omer, no weddings are held. On Lag Ba'omer, however, the day the plague ended, it is permitted to conduct a wedding ceremony or any other celebration.

Lag Ba'omer is a half-holiday. It comes, in May, on the 33d day of the counting of the Omer. The Hebrew letter "L" is the numeral for 30; "G" is the numeral for 3. Lag Ba'omer therefore means the 33d day of the Omer.

Another Sage of that period, Rabbi Simon Ben Yochai, called Bar Yochai, defied the Romans by establishing a network of schools throughout the land. The Romans sought to kill him. He escaped to hide in a cave. On Lag Ba'omer the children came to him to continue their studies. That is why Lag Ba'omer is also treated as a children's holiday. They celebrate by going on outings and picnics, recalling the actions of those children who went out to the fields to Bar Yochai to study the Torah.

SHAVUOTH (*The holiday of weeks*)

According to the Torah, seven weeks must be counted off, from Passover to Shavuoth, which falls on the sixth and seventh days of the month of Sivan (May-June). Shavuoth is celebrated for two days. In Israel it is celebrated for one day only. Shavuoth is known too, as the holiday of the gathering of first fruit (Chag Habikurim). On that holiday, in ancient Israel, the Jews from all parts of the land, presented their first fruits to the Temple. It is also called the Holiday of the Giving of the Torah (Zman Matan Toratenu). Tradition tells us that on that day Moses received the Tablets of the Torah from God on Mt. Sinai.

AKDOMOT   This is a poem in praise of God, read on Shavuoth, in the synagogue.

MEGILATH RUTH (The scroll of Ruth)   On Shavuoth the beautiful story of Ruth, great-grandmother of King David, is read. A Moabite princess, she married a Jew in the land of Moab. When he died, she turned her back on a life of luxury in Moab to return with her mother-in-law Naomi, to Israel. Choosing a life of poverty in preference to giving up her religion and principles, she became the symbol of loyalty and piety.

SPECIAL DISHES EATEN ON SHAVUOTH

Blintzes: A cheese pastry usually eaten on Shavuoth, the holiday celebrating the giving of the Torah and the Summer harvest in Israel. They symbolize the Torah as being as good as milk. They also symbolize the land of Israel which was once a land flowing with milk and honey.

Teiglach: Candies made with honey and eaten on Shavuoth (and also on Rosh Hashanah, to denote a sweet year) to signify that the Torah is sweet as honey.

Shaltenoses: Boiled blintzes eaten cold on Shavuoth, mostly by Jews of Lithuania, as it originated there. The word "Shalte" is Lithuanian, meaning cold.

ROSH CHODESH (*beginning of the month*)

The beginning of each month is considered a half-holiday. Rosh Chodesh is sometimes observed for one day, sometimes for two days, depending upon the calendar. Prayers are said, as on other holidays, except that the first half of the service is drawn from midweek services and the other half from holiday services. Hallel is included. Hallel (meaning praise), consists of a number of psalms praising God.

TISHA B'AV (*Nine days in Ab*)

Tisha B'av is a day of mourning, for on that day both the first and the second Temples were destroyed. Tisha B'av is observed by fasting for twenty-four hours and by reading the scroll of Eicha. This scroll contains the lamentations of the prophet Jeremiah, who witnessed the destruction of the first Temple. Also Kinot, or special lamentations, are chanted in the Synagogue.

Tisha B'av is also the day on which the Jews were expelled from Spain in 1492, the same day Columbus set sail on the voyage which resulted in his discovery of America.

OTHER FAST DAYS

Besides the fasts of Gedaliah, of Esther and Tisha B'av there are other fast days. Some of them are:

ASARAH B'TEVETH (ten days in the month of Teveth).
On this day the Babylonians laid siege to Jerusalem.

SHIVAH ASAR B'TAMUZ (seventeen days in the month of Tamuz). Tamuz precedes the month of Ab. This day commemorates the following events:

1. Moses smashed the Tablets on finding the Israelites worshipping the Golden Calf, when he brought the Tablets down from Mt. Sinai.
2. Ending of the daily sacrifices in the Temple as a result of the famine in Jerusalem during the siege by the Babylonians.
3. The conquering army of Babylon entered Jerusalem on the 17th day of Tamuz.

CHAPTER TWELVE

MODERN JEWISH CULTURE

THE EIGHTEENTH AND NINETEENTH CENTURIES IN JEWISH CULTURAL LIFE

Modern Hebrew Culture began with the Haskalah (enlightenment) movement in the 18th and 19th Centuries. This movement advocated secular education for Jews in a Jewish national spirit. The Haskalites or Maskilim advocated the use of the Hebrew language not only for prayer but for daily speech and literary expression.

The father of the Haskalah movement could be considered Moses Mendelssohn, the philosopher. His followers, Marcus Hertz and David Friedlander, however, went too far with their enlightenment, and the result was the conversion to Christianity of many of their followers.

The first part of the Haskalah period (1781-1820), was called the "Me'asef" period, after the name of the Haskalah monthly journal called by that name (Me'asef means gatherer). In the journal, assimilationism was preached.

A second group of Haskalah writers gathered around the *Bikure-Ha'itim* journal, which was the Austrian center of Haskalah. It was founded on the initiative of Shalom Hakohen, and continued to circulate annually for twelve years (1820-1831).

In Galicia, there sprang up a separate group. Among the

Maskilim, there were such people as Joseph Perl (1773-1839), a great satirist; Isaac Erter and others, like the poet Meir Letteris. The father of the Haskalah movement in Russia is considered to be Isaac Baer Levinson (1788-1860). H was known for his books, *Beth-Yehudah*, in which he explained to the Czarist government the essentials of Judaism; *Efes Damim*, which proves effectively the foolishness of the blood accusation against Jews, and *Zerubabel*, a book in defense of the Talmud.

One of the initiators of the Haskalah movement in Russia was Mordecai Aaron Ginzberg (1796-1847), who established it at Wilna, Lithuania. To that group belonged such great men as Abraham Dob Lebenson, known under his pen name of Adam. He was a talented poet. His son, Micah Joseph Lebenson, was also known as a great poet. Judah Leib Gordon (1831-1895), was known as a great poet, novelist and active Haskalah fighter. He was one of the editors of the Ha'Melitz daily.

Other important Russian Maskilim were:

Abraham Mapu (1808-1868), who wrote the first novel in modern Hebrew Literature, *Ahavat Zion* (*The love of Zion*). He also wrote the famous *Ait Zabua* (*The Hypocrite*), and *Ashmat Shomron* (*The Sin of Shomron*).

Peretz Smolenskin (1842-1885), who became the dominant figure of the Haskalah movement in his time, due to his novels. He published the Hebrew monthly *Ha'Shachar* (*The Dawn*), in which he published most of his novels, like *Hatoeh B'Darche Ha'Chaim* and others. He was the first to begin a spiritual revival in Jewish literature.

Moses Leib Lilienbloom is famous for his novel *Hatat Neurim* (*Sins of Youth*), and for his militant attitude for the cause of Haskalah.

Also known were Kalman Shulman, Reuben Broydes and others.

There were a number of writers who tried to introduce in the Haskalah movement a considerable number of scientific books. Such writers were Chaim Slonimsky, Joseph Schoenback, the historian Henrich Graetz, Samuel David Luzzato, Leopold Zunz, Solomon Rappoport, Nachman Krochmal, Shalom Abramowitz, who later became famous as Mendele Mocher Sefarim. The Maskilim formed groups around periodicals. Besides the Me'asef, Bikure-Ha'itim and the Ha'Shachar, there were the Hamagid group with the *Ha'Tzofeh* (*The Observer*), the *Ha'Carmel,* and the *Ha'Melitz* (*The Advocate*) founded by Alexander Zederbaum in Odessa, Russia, in 1860.

While the Haskalah was developing, the leaders in religious learning made real strides in their literary work. In 1837 Moses Landau published the *Biur* (*Explanation*), a translation of the Tanach with all its commentaries. Rabbi Meir Lebush Malbim wrote a commentary on the entire Tanach, also a number of other books. Isaac Hirsh Weiss (19th Century), wrote: *Dor Dor Ve'dorshov* (*Each Generation with its Scholars*), a history of Jewish tradition. Gustav Karpeles wrote a history of Jewish literature. Rabbi Israel Lifshitz wrote the *Tiferet Israel* (*Glory of Israel*), a simple commentary on the Mishna. Joseph Teomin wrote the *Peri-Megadim* (*Sweet Fruits*), a commentary on the Shulchan Aruch part of Yoreh Dea. The *Kezot-Ha-Hoshen,* a commentary on the

Shulchan Aruch book of Hoshen Mishpat, was written by
Ari Leib Cohen. The still popular code, the *Hayeh-Adam*
(*Life of Man*) and *Chochmat Adam* (*Wisdom of Man*),
written by Rabbi Abraham Danzig (1748-1820) of Wilna,
pupil of Rabbi Ezekiel Landau, the great Talmudist known
under the name of Nodah Biyehudah. There were also written
at that time, the *Responsas* of Rabbi Akiba Eiger and of
Rabbi Moses Sofer, known under the name of Hatam Sofer,
who was the son-in-law of Rabbi Eiger and *Responsas* by
Rabbi Isaac Elchanan Spector (1817-1896), Rabbi of Kovno,
Lithuania. There were also a number of ethical books written
by the most popular preacher of his time, Jacob Kranz, world
famous as the Dubner Maggid (18th Century), or preacher.
There were many more too numerous to mention.

The Twentieth Century in Jewish Cultural Life

In the twentieth Century, the Haskalah movement produced
writers and leaders with a realistic and psychological view-
point. The best known of them were:

David Frishman, who analyzes the mental and emotional
state of his heroes.

Mordecai Feierberg, who described in his stories the con-
trasting viewpoints in the life of the Jew.

Judah Steinberg, also a great short story writer, as was
S. Gutman, known by his pen-name of Ben-Zion.

Ben Avigdor, Isaiah Bershadski, Chaim Brenner (who was
killed in Palestine in 1921, fighting against the Arabs),
I. Berkowitz, Micah Berdichevsky, A. Singer, J. L. Katzenelson, Mendel Dolitzky, Z. Maneh, H. Imber, and others,
were also talented writers and poets.

Chaim Nachman Bialik (1873-1934), is considered the greatest modern Hebrew poet. His poem *El Hatzipor* (*To the Bird*) revealed his great talents. His *Hamathmid* (*The Diligent Student*), his *Ha'Shechita* (*The Slaughter*), the *Megilath Ha'Esh* (*Scroll of Fire*) and many others, made him the most important Hebrew national poet of the twentieth century. He later settled in Israel, where he became a publisher.

Saul Tzernichovsky is also considered among the great poets. By profession a physician, he devoted most of his time to writing.

The third to be considered among the great three, is Zalman Shneur.

The distinguished writers and publicists of that period were Nahum Sokolow, considered the theoretician of the Zionist movement, Reuben Brainin and Joseph Klausner.

There was also a Ha'Shiloach group of writers, centered around the Hebrew monthly magazine *Ha'Shiloach*, founded by Ahad Ha'am, a Zionist nationalist, and founder of the Zionist movement of Ahad-Ha'Amism. To that group belonged: I. Rabnitzky, Mordecai Erenpreis, the great Zionist speaker Shemarya Levin, Joshua Thon, who later became a member of the Polish Senate, and a number of others.

There was another group of writers, who centered themselves around the Zionist weekly, the *Haolam* (*the World*). Those who belonged to that group were: Alter Druyanov (1880-1938), Moses Kleinman, Bar Tubia, Hillel Zeitlin, Samuel Leib Zitron, and others.

In the religious literature of the century, Baruch Epstein wrote his *Torah Temima* (*A Complete Torah*), Nachman

Bialik and J. Rabnitzky compiled the *Sefer Ha'Agada,* an anthology of Agada literature. J. Katzenelson wrote the *Hatalmud V'harefuah (The Talmud and Medicine).* A translation of the Talmud into German by Lazarus Goldsschmidt, and the *Fundamentals of Jewish Law* by Asher Gulak were also written.

Among the Jewish historians of the 20th Century, no doubt, Simon Doubnow takes the first place. Other historians are Joseph Klausner, A. Tzerikover, Solomon Rosanes, S. Horodetzky, Nahum Sokolow, who wrote the *History of Zionism,* and others.

Among those who wrote histories of Jewish Literature are Fishel Liachover and J. Klausner.

In Philosophy, Religion and Ethics, the best known are Moses Hess of the 19th Century, Rabbi Zevi Hirsh Kalisher, father of Spiritual Zionism, Ahad Ha'am, Martin Buber, A. Gordon, Herman Cohen, Moritz Lazarus, Abraham Isaac Cook, (late Chief Rabbi of Palestine) and a number of others.

In Palestine, the cradle of Jewish religious and ethical culture, the twentieth Century brought forth a new modern Hebrew literature, which in turn brought a revival of the Hebrew language.

Among the best known writers are:

The belletrist A. Kabak, the writers M. Kimchi, Asher Barash, Avigdor Hameiri, Samuel Agnon, Judah Burlo, Eber Hadani, Moshe Smilanski, Eliezer Steinman, and others.

Among the best Palestinian poets are, Abraham Shlonsky, Avigdor Hameiri, Uri Grenberg, the famous Elisheba, who was a Russian woman, but settled in Palestine and became not only the adopted daughter of Israel but also contributed beautiful poetry in Israel's own language, Hebrew. Many other writers, dramatists, and poets are contributing to the ever-growing Israeli literature.

YIDDISH LITERATURE

Yiddish is the language spoken by the Jews of Eastern Europe. It is based on German with a mixture of Hebrew and the local languages such as English, Russian, Polish, French, depending upon where the community lived.

Yiddish literature began to develop in the nineteenth century when Zederbaum, the publisher of the Hebrew *Hamelitz,* began to publish the first Yiddish weekly, the *Kol Mevaser.* It was also at that time, that Shalom Abramowitz (1835-1917), the Hebrew writer, decided to reach the masses and introduce the Haskalah by means of the Yiddish language. He was one of the three literary lions of Yiddish, the other two being Isaac Leib Peretz and Shalom Aleichem. He soon became known as Mendele Mocher Seforim. There were a number of Yiddish writers before him, like Israel Axenfield, Solomon Ettinger, Isaac Dick and others, but Mendele Mocher Seforim is the one who really made Yiddish literature develop on a national scale and put it among the other great literatures. This is particularly true of his novels, *The Kliatche (The Horse)* and the *Taxeh (The Tax Box).*

The second of the lions of Yiddish literature was Isaac Leib Peretz. At first he contributed to the magazine *Ha'asif,* in Hebrew. He then turned to Yiddish, and wrote many Hasidic stories which to this day are extremely popular.

The third giant of Yiddish literature was the great humorist

Shlomo Rabinowich, better known throughout the Jewish world (and as a result of many translations, the non-Jewish world) as Shalom Aleichem. His stories and dramas are still popular and widely read. His *Tevyeh der Milchiger* (*Tevyeh the Dairyman*), *Motel Peise dem Chazzn's* (*Motel, the son of the Chazzan*), *Blonzende Shteren* (*Wandering Stars*) and many others, have enriched greatly both Yiddish literature and, through translations, all of world literature. He is regarded as the Yiddish Mark Twain; indeed, it is said that when Mark Twain was introduced to Shalom Aleichem, the humorist writer referred to himself as the English "Shalom Aleichem."

Other writers in Yiddish were Mordecai Spector, Abraham Reisen, H. Nomberg, Shalom Ash (whose works are world famous), David Regelson, Simon Frug, who wrote poems in Yiddish and in Russian, David Pinsky, Leon Kobrin, Yehoash (famous for his translation of the Bible in Yiddish), Opatoshu and others.

In the period of extensive Jewish immigration to the United States, there emerged a large Jewish press and Jewish theater that ranked with the best in the world. The first Yiddish newspaper in America was established by Sarnson. Two of the outstanding Jewish dailies to mention are: *The Jewish Morning Journal-Day* and the *Jewish Daily Forward* with circulations in the hundreds of thousands. Both the press and the theater remain impressive to this day.

ARCHITECTURE

When Moses directed Bezalel (approx. 1300 B.C.E.) and his Egyptian-trained assistants to build the Tabernacle according to God's own instructions to Moses, it appeared that the birth of a distinctive Hebrew architecture was at hand. However, invasions by powerful enemies time and again, prevented this development, superimposing instead, their own tastes and styles. Consequently architecture in Israel shifted from Canaanite and Philistine to Egyptian and Phoenician design. Then, in order, came Assyrian, Babylonian, Persian, Greek and Roman influences.

Even King Solomon's intensive building was carried out by foreign experts. Many hundreds of palaces and other structures were built for Solomon, his 300 wives and others connected with his court. Most of his wives were foreign princesses, and exerted their own native tastes on architecture.

Today, there are many Jewish designers and architects actively working and creating all over the world. At present, in Israel, architects are adapting the best qualities of European, American and Asian architecture and engineering. It is expected that in the near future a specific Israeli art form will develop in these fields.

Sculpture and Painting

The art of sculpture and painting took no root in Jewish communities until modern times. This was due to the Second Commandment which expressly forbids the making of images or likenesses of any object or organism existing on land, in the air or in the sea. But these Art forms only lay dormant. In modern times, there are many fine Jewish artists like Antokolsky in Russia, and Epstein in England, and painters like Chagall, Szyk, Maniewitz, Mayerowitz, Soyer, Jack Levine, Chaim Gross, William Gropper and others.

MUSIC AND DANCE

In the field of music and dance the Jews can more successfully lay claim to a national form and national originality.
Several historical biblical facts bear this out:

MIRIAM   After the successful crossing of the Red Sea (1300
B.C.E.), Moses' sister Miriam and other women took cymbals
and danced in praise of God.

INSTRUMENTS   In the Tabernacle and in the Temples, the
Levites played on instruments which included the horn, tim-
brel, pipe, clear-toned cymbals, loud-sounding cymbals, the
harp, the lyre and other string instruments.

KING DAVID'S COURT   The Jews developed their own melodies
and songs as typified by the songs and instrumental music in
King David's court.

MUSICAL NOTATION   It is believed that about 600 C.E., the
Ta'ame Hanegina or musical notation was instituted, although some ancient Mishna writings had musical notations
in them. Each symbol represents melodic phrases or musical
intervals. To this day, the system is used in the chanting of
the Torah and the Prophets. All that is lacking in this system
of musical notation is the key signature and specific starting
pitch.

NUSACH   After the destruction of the second Temple, specific and intensive Nusachim or liturgical forms of composition and melody were originated in connection with special
religious prayers and services. Two thousand years of wandering over the face of the globe has, no doubt, added considerably to the repertoire, but it remains essentially traditional.

For Jew and non-Jew alike it stands as a highly respected art form.

ZEMIROTH   In the Diaspora there originated the custom of Zemiroth, group singing of attractive, joyous and haunting melodies, during and at the end of meals. The melodies were introduced by the Hasidic Rabbis who claimed that song brings man nearer to God. What such singing does for relaxation, peace of mind, creating desirable moods and facilitating digestion of food, can be best attested to by modern medical and psychological authorities.

DANCING created and developed in the 18th and 19th Centuries by Hasidic students. These Hasidim became famous for their expressiveness and gestures in the dance.

MUSICIANS   The number of great musicians and composers of Jewish faith or heritage is legion. Names such as Mendelssohn, Saint Saens, Meyerbeer, Mahler, Copland, Gershwin, Bernstein, and Rubenstein, Horowitz, Heifitz, Szigetti, Elman are known throughout the world. Four composers of international reputation—Schoenberg, Castelnuovo-Tedesco, Bloch, and Milhaud—have written works specifically for the synagogue, and many others have written works based on national or folk themes. Among these latter are Paul Ben Haim, Jacob Weinberg, Marc Lavry, Joel Engel, Hanock Jacoby, and Josef Tal, all of whose music has a distinctly national or religious flavor.

At present in Israel, great stress is laid on the Music, Dance, Drama and literary art forms. Already important contributions to international culture are being made from Israel, the newest fountain-head of culture.

APPENDIX

Hebrew Names and Their English Meanings

AARON singing mountain
ABBA father
ABIGAIL father's joy
ABNER father of light
ABRAHAM father of nations
ABSALOM father of peace
ADAM made of earth
ADINA refined
AMOS to load
AMRAM exalted nation
ARI or ARIEYEH lion
ASHER lucky one
AZRIEL God helps

BARAK lightning
BARUCH blessed
BATHIA daughter of God
BENJAMIN right-hand man
BEN ZION son of Zion
BERACHA blessing
BERURIA woman selected by God
BESSIE daughter of God

CHAIM life

DAN or DINAH judge
DANIEL God will judge
DAVID beloved
DEBORAH bee
DEVASHA honey
DOV bear

ELIAHU God is the Lord
ELIAKIM God shall confirm
ELIAS God is the Lord
ELIEZER God's help
ELISHA God shall save
ELIZA happy
ELKANAH bought by God
EPHRAIM multiply
ESTHER name of Persian goddess of love (Istahar)
EZEKIEL God is strong
EZRA help
EVA mother of living

GABRIEL God's strength
GAD good luck
GAMALIEL God recompensed me
GERSHOM a stranger there

HADASSAH   myrtle
HANNAH   favored one
HANOCH   educated
HILLEL   praised
HOSEA   help

ISAAC   to laugh
ISAIAH   God shall save
ISHMAEL   God shall hear
ISRAEL   one who fought with
   a prince of God

JACOB   heel
JEHOSAPHAT   God judged
JEPHTAH   shall open
JEREMIAH   God is exalted
JEROBOAM   quarreler
JOAB   God is father
JOEL   the Lord is God
JONAH   dove
JONATHAN   God gave
JOSEPH   shall add
JOSHUA   God shall save
JUDAH   give thanks
JUDITH   same as Judah

LEAH   weary one
LEVI   to join

MALKA   queen
MARGALIT   pearl
MEIR   gives light

MELECH   king
MENUCHA   rest
MICHAEL   who is like God
MIRIAM   the elated one
MOSES   extricated from
   water

NADAV   charitable
NACHMAN   comforter
NAFTALI   fighter
NAOMI   pleasant
NATHAN   gave
NATHANIEL   given by God
NEHEMIAH   comforted by
   God
NOAH   pleasant

OBADIAH   servant of God

PENINA   precious

RACHEL   ewe
RAFAEL   God heals
REBECCA   pleasant association
REUBEN   see a son
RINA or RONA   song
RUTH   religious zealot

SAADIA   sustained by God
SAMUEL   God listened
SARAH   princess

SAUL asking or having borrowed
SHACHNA good neighbor
SHALOM peace
SHEMARIAH God watches
SHIFRA beautifier
SHOSHANA rose
SHULAMIT woman of peace
SHRAGA a candle
SIMCHA happiness
SIMON God heard
SOLOMON man of peace

TAMAR palm tree
TIRZA favored
TOBIAS or TUVIAH God is good

TZILA shadow
TZIVIA a female deer; an attractive woman

YAFFA beautiful
YISSACHAR good price
YECHIEL living God
YERUCHAM God pities
YOCHEVED honored by God

ZADOK just
ZALMAN man of peace
ZECHARIAH God remembers
ZEHAVA of gold
Z'EV wolf
ZIONA to Zion
ZIPPORAH bird

Bibliography

	Translation by Alexander Harkavi, pub-
The Pentateuch	lished by Hebrew Publishing Co., New
The Prophets	York, 1934.
The Hagiographa	Also by Chief Rabbi of Britain, Dr.
	Hertz, published in London, England.

Abrahams, Israel, *Jewish Life in the Middle Ages,* Jewish Publication Society, Philadelphia, 1911.

Adler, Elkan N., *Jewish Travelers,* London, 1930.

Ausubel, Nathan, *A Treasury of Jewish Folklore,* Crown Publishers, New York, 1948-1954.

Baron, Salo W., *A Social and Religious History of the Jews,* New York, Columbia University, 1937.

Baron, Salo W., *The Jewish Community,* 3 volumes, Jewish Publication Society, Philadelphia, 1942.

Buber, Martin, *Tales of the Hasidim,* Shocken Books, 1947.

Cohen, A., *Everyman's Talmud,* London, 1937.

Cohen, I., *Jewish Life in Modern Times,* Dodd, Mead, New York, 1914.

Danby, H., *The Mishna,* London, 1933.

Dubnow, Simon M., *An Outline of Jewish History,* 3 volumes, published by Max Maisel, New York, 1925.

Freedman, Lee M., *Jewish Pioneers and Patriots,* Jewish Publication Society, Philadelphia, 1942.

Ginzberg, Louis, *The Legends of the Jews,* 7 volumes, Jewish Publication Society, Philadelphia, 1938.

Goldin, Hyman E., *Text of the Talmud,* The Jordan Publishing Co., New York, 1933.

Goldin, Hyman E., *The Book of Legends,* 3 volumes, The Jordan Publishing Co., New York, 1929.

Grayzel, Solomon, *A History of the Jews,* Jewish Publication Society, Philadelphia, 1948.

Greenstone, J. H., *The Messiah Idea in Jewish History,* Jewish Publication Society, Philadelphia, 1906.

Horodetzky, S., *Leaders of Hasidism,* London, 1928.

Jacobs, Joseph, *Jewish Contributions to Civilization,* Jewish Publication Society, Philadelphia, 1919.

Janovsky, Oscar I., *The American Jew,* Harper, New York, 1942.

Learsi, Rufus, *The Book of Jewish Humor,* Bloch, New York, 1941.

Lebeson, Anita, *Jewish Pioneers in America,* New York, Brentano, 1931.

Millgram, Abraham E., *An Anthology of Medieval Hebrew Literature,* Associated Talmud Torahs, Philadelphia, 1935.

Newman, Louis I., *The Hasidic Anthology,* Scribner's, New York, 1938.

Radin, Max, *The Jews Among the Greeks and Romans,* Jewish Publication Society, Philadelphia, 1915.

Raisin, Jacob S., *The Haskalah Movement in Russia,* Jewish Publication Society, Philadelphia, 1913.

Revutzky, Abraham, *Jews in Palestine,* Vanguard Press, New York, 1936.

Richman, Jacob, *Laughs From Jewish Lore,* Behrman's Jewish Book House, New York, 1939.

Roback, A. A., *The History of Yiddish Literature,* Yivo, New York, 1940.

Sachar, A. L., *A History of the Jews,* New York, Knopf, 1940.

Salaman, Nina and Brody, *Selected Poems of Yehudah Halevi,* Jewish Publication Society, Philadelphia, 1928.

Samuel, Maurice, *The World of Sholom Aleichem,* Knopf, New York, 1944.

Schwartz, Leo W., *The Jewish Caravan,* Farrar and Rinehart, New York, 1935.

Teitelbaum, Elsa, *An Anthology of Jewish Humor and Maxims,* Pardes Publishing Co., New York, 1945.

Waxman, Meyer, *A History of Jewish Literature,* 4 volumes, New York, Bloch, 1941.

Wiernik, Peter, *History of the Jews in America,* Jewish Press Publishing Co., New York, 1912.

ADDENDA

THE JEWS OF ENGLAND

England erred badly in her treatment of Jews during their struggle for a national home, for Jews might have been satisfied with dominion status and probably would have remained steadfast friends of England forever. But in trying to play the Arabs off against Jews, England not only lost the Jews, but the Arabs sided with Germany during World War II. The result was that England had to get out of the Middle East as well as Palestine, thus giving up the rich land with its vital oil deposits. England never regained her prestige or power after that.

THE JEWS OF RUSSIA

Although Russia was the second among the world's great powers to recognize the new state of Israel, what Stalin really had in mind was to keep the British out of the Middle East. By supplying Israel with ammunition and arms in her fight against the Arabs, he hoped to gain her support in the ever-growing "Cold War." When, however, Israel sided with the United States and Stalin saw his "investment" go down the drain, he changed his policy overnight and Russia reverted to her old anti-Semitic ways. Thousands of Jews were sent to concentration camps in Siberia and many more thousands were killed outright, as in the days of Old Russia. The Soviet Union became the chief purveyor of anti-Semitic poison throughout the world, and remains the chief oppressor of Jews in the world today. The same thing is happening in the Eastern Bloc countries allied to the Soviet Union.

The Jews of Egypt

Egypt and Israel clashed again in 1956-57 (Sinai Campaign) and in 1967 when, in a lightning campaign, Israel's forces occupied the whole of the Sinai Peninsula (June 5-10, "The 6-Day War"). The war ended with a cease-fire but Israel continued to occupy the captured territories.

In 1977, Egyptian president Anwar Sadat suddenly decided to make peace with Israel, in return for which Israel would give up the Sinai. He flew to Jerusalem, spoke to the Knesset, and, at the urging of President Carter of the United States, signed a peace treaty with Israel. Despite the assassination of President Sadat in 1981 by Egyptian dissidents, it is hoped that the initiative he took will prove to be a breakthrough in the difficult negotiations for peace between Israel and her Arab neighbors.

The Jews of Ethiopia

At present, Ethiopia is under communist rule, and as many Falashas as can manage it are trying to save themselves by fleeing to Israel.

Economy, Industry, Agriculture

The Israeli Postal System now has offices in practically every town, village, yishuv, and hamlet, be it Jewish or Arab. It provides most services that are provided in any industrialized country, and it also receives and makes payments on behalf of the Government and National Insurance Institute. The telephone system has direct telegraphic communications with most of the world. Direct calls can be placed from Jerusalem to New York, California, or London, and vice versa. Some of Israel's banks have multi-billion-dollar assets and branches all over the world.

SOCIAL WELFARE

In addition to the Hadassah and the Kupat Cholim hospitals and clinics, there are also the great Sha'arei Tzedek Hospital in Jerusalem, Beilinson's Hospital in Tel Aviv, and a number of others. The Number of clinics has nearly doubled since 1953, and all facilities are equipped with the most modern medical equipment.

HIGHLIGHTS IN THE HISTORY OF ISRAEL

The days of Abraham and Jacob	Seventeenth-sixteenth centuries, B.C.E.
The Conquest of Canaan	Thirteenth century B.C.E.
David makes Jerusalem the capital	1000 B.C.E.
Solomon builds the Temple	960 B.C.E.
The kingdom is divided	930 B.C.E.
Israel conquered by Assyria	721 B.C.E.
Judah conquered by Babylon	586 B.C.E.
The return from Babylon and building of the Second Temple	538-515 B.C.E.
The return of Ezra and Nehemiah	457-424 B.C.E.
The period of Greek rule	323-168 B.C.E.
The Maccabee revolt	168 B.C.E.
Roman rule begins	63 B.C.E.
The reign of King Herod	37-4 B.C.E.-C.E.
Destruction of the Second Temple	70 C.E.
The revolt at Massada	73 C.E.
The Bar Kochba revolt	132 C.E.
The completion of the Mishna	200 C.E.

The revolt against Rome	352 C.E.
The completion of the Talmud	500 C.E.
Arab rule begins	636 C.E.
The period of the Crusaders' rule	1099-1291 C.E.
The Turkish conquest	1517 C.E.
The first Aliyah	1882 C.E.
The first Zionist Congress	1897 C.E.
The second Aliyah	1904-1914 C.E.
The founding of Tel-Aviv	1909 C.E.
The Balfour Declaration	1917 C.E.
The third Aliyah	1920 C.E.
The period of British mandate	1922-1948
Transjordan separated from Palestine	1922
Hebrew University on Mount Scopus opened	1925
Israel's independence proclaimed	May 14, 1948
Israel attacked by five Arab armies	May 15, 1948
Elections to first Knesset	January 25, 1949
Chaim Weitzman elected first President	February 16, 1949
Israel admitted to United Nations	May 11, 1949
Opening of Weitzman Institute of Science	November 2, 1949
Yitzchak Ben Zvi becomes President	December 8, 1952
Oil discovered in Heletz	September 22, 1955
The Sinai war with Egypt	October 29, 1956
First atomic reactor activated	July 4, 1960
The construction of Port Ashdod begins	July 30, 1960
Zalman Shazar becomes President	May 21, 1963
New Knesset building opened in Jerusalem	August 30, 1966
The Six-Day War begins	June 5, 1967
Jerusalem reunited	June 29, 1967
Yom Kippur War	October 5, 1973
Anwar Sadat visits Jerusalem	November 19, 1977
Camp David Peace Treaty between Egypt and Israel signed	17 September 1978

Index